INDO-THAI HISTORICAL AND CULTURAL LINKAGES

INDO-THAI HISTORICAL AND CULTURAL LINKAGES

Edited by

Neeru Misra and Sachchidanand Sahai

MANOHAR
2007

First published 2007

ISBN 81-7304-757-X

Published by
Ajay Kumar Jain for
Manohar Publishers & Distributors
4753/23 Ansari Road, Daryaganj
New Delhi 110002

Printed at
Lordson Publishers Pvt. Ltd.
Delhi 110007

Contents

Second Seminar of Indo-Thai Historical and Cultural Linkages 21-23 August 2006 Bangkok, Thailand

ORGANIZED BY THE ROYAL THAI EMBASSY, NEW DELHI AND THE INDIAN COUNCIL FOR CULTURAL RELATIONS, NEW DELHI

The Royal Thai Embassy, New Delhi, in collaboration with the Indian Council for Cultural Relations, held a seminar on Indo-Thai historical and cultural linkages to explore the age-old relationship between the two countries, and its contribution to the formation of a global Asian civilization and consciousness in today's world. The seminar held from 21 to 23 August 2006, in Bangkok, Thailand, was the second of its kind, the first having been held in New Delhi in 2005.

The seminar saw two days of involved debate and deliberations by leading academics from both the countries. The various sessions focused on varied topics, all of which contributed to a consolidated discussion at the end. The last day, 23 August, was devoted to an educative and entertaining trip to Ayutthiya and other stops along the way. This helped the Indian delegation to understand Thai ways and culture better.

21 AUGUST 2006

Inaugural Session

The Seminar was inaugurated by Mr. Chirasak Thanesnant, Ambassador of the Royal Thai Embassy, India. In his opening remarks the Ambassador said he felt privileged to be in the midst of such eminent people to foster and further Indo-Thai relations. Making a brief mention of the first seminar, he mooted again the idea, first discussed in 2004, of establishing a Thai Cultural Centre in India. He stressed the warm relationship shared by the Royal Thai Embassy and the Indian Council for Cultural Relations, and said that in order to keep the momentum of the project alive, alternate seminars were a must. These could be held in New Delhi and Bangkok. This would enable the two countries to explore the historical and cultural relations that have existed between them for more than 2000 years. The most vital aim for this second seminar was, according to him, a concrete plan for the establishment of a Thai Cultural Centre in India.

Mr. T.P.P. Seetharam, Deputy Chief of Mission, Embassy of India, Thailand, representing the Indian Embassy, Bangkok, read out a message from the Director General, ICCR. He added that Indians travel to Thailand as tourists unaware of the historical links between the countries. Thai words have resonances from Sanskrit and Malayalam but very few can explain the significance of these linkages. Today names like Tata Young or *Dhoom*, the movie, are popular as are the ones in the fields of IT and biotechnology. While links between Bangalore and Bangkok have immediate resonance, especially to the younger generations, the old links should be explored again.

Mr. Piyawat Niyomrerks, the Deputy Permanent Secretary of the Ministry of Foreign Affairs, Thailand, extended his welcome to all, and said that Thailand was proud of its history and heritage. Thailand's 'Look West' policy blends well with India's 'Look East' policy. The people of India and Thailand need to know each other better. Thailand would like the trade to increase; to have cooperation in various sectors of energy; and to have open skies and port linkages. The Thai Government has tried to strengthen these bonds and in a seminar like this it is taken further by the peoples, supplementing government's efforts.

1ST SESSION: THAI HERITAGE SITES

The First Session on Thai Heritage Sites was moderated by Chirapat Prapandvidya. The first speaker, Phasook Indrawooth spoke on the Dvaravati. Evidence has been found to show the connections between Dvaravati and India. A map showing trade contacts between India (Patliputra) and the west, the sea routes, numismatic evidences, etched beads, seals, combs, dice, ivory (bearing Sanskrit, early Brahmi and Prakrit words), and silver coins found at the site bearing symbols of fertility all establish the richness of linkages. The concepts of state and kinship in Dvaravati show Indian ideas. In a predominantly Buddhist kingdom traces of Hindu religion were found. Phasook Indrawooth showed a number of slides to illustrate his argument.

Prof. Satyavrat Shastri spoke mainly of three heritage parks of the Sukhothai, which have Brahmanical artefacts housed in Bangkok.

Amara Srisuchat elaborated on these world heritage sites in Thailand which reflect Indo-Thai cultural linkages. She mentioned how Ban Chiang was declared protected by the UNESCO in 1991. She also gave details about the Sukhothai and associated cities, like Ayutthiya, with an overview and maps. She gave names and dates of Hindu shrines in the Sukhothai and listed out the similarities.

Kishor Kumar Basa spoke on 'Celebrating the Indo-Thai Cultural Heritage: Some Issues and Challenges for the Thai Cultural Centre'. He gave details of evidence of contact between the two countries, which can be seen especially in the Mutisala beads, knobbed vessels, and tin-bronze articles from India. He referred to the period of transition and the era of globalization that has emerged to dominate us. He warned that issues of archaeology and museology had to move away from Western notions.

Parul Pandya Dhar spoke on the *Prasada* (Prasat) in India and Thailand: Cultural Transformations. She said that the *Prasada*—royal palace, house of god, or sacred sanctuary—has a long conceptual and morphological evolution, development, and transformation in the South and South-East Asian regions. *Prasada* of the northern India textual tradition is more commonly encountered as *vimana* in the southern Indian Texts. The idea and the image of the *prasada* further find parallel expressions in the Khmer Prasat of present-day Cambodia and Thailand.

Amarjeeva Lochan spoke on the Thai in India: Problem and Adjustments. He mentioned the long relationship between the countries. The first recorded visit of a Thai pilgrim to India was of Monak Srisraddha Ratna Lankaradipa who visited Cholamandalam (Tamil Nadu). Of course, references are not always found of all the visits. In modern times many Thai students have come to India but the scene changed after the Vietnam disaster. India has awarded 500 Doctorate degress to Thai students, the highest for any country.

Since 1972, tourism has increased, as well as religious visits to Rajgriha, Gaya, and Nalanda. Delicious Thai cuisine is now quite popular in India. Lochan made mention of the Annual Bangkok Meeting of Thai alumni from India, and spoke of the problems faced by the Thai students. Coming to India, according to him, was easy for the Thai, rather than going to USA, since language and cultural sharing was easier.

The session ended with some questions and answers and with the moderator reasserting that the Thai scholars should give their inputs and suggestions for the Thai Cultural Centre.

2ND SESSION: PHILOSOPHY OF LIFE: BUDDHISM IN PRACTICE TODAY

The second session was moderated by Prof. Nongluk Thepswas. The first speaker, Rana Purushottam Kumar Singh spoke on the 'Theory of Mind in Early Buddhist Philosophy', defining what Buddhistology means today. He said that the mind has the capacity to calm to nervous system of the body. Avidharma is not only a science but a philosophy. According to Buddhist philosophy the mind is dynamic. A reinterpretation of Avidharma is required to use and understand feelings based on consciousness.

Charan Thongasen, who joined the session, said that Buddhism is not a dogma, but a philosophy required for creative thinking. It is a way or pattern of life for one who understands the reality of life and righteousness, without depending on the supernatural. Buddhism helps in self-realization, self-enquiry and analysis through which happiness can be attained. It suggests a practical method by spontaneous action and creative thinking. Life is full of suffering and the mind is essential to humanity. With our thoughts we make the world, our life. To understand the mind would mean to understand Buddhist teaching. Buddhist practice is related to holy practice.

Ravindra Panth began by saying that 2006 was an auspicious year due to the Mahaparinirvan of Buddha. History is the root while culture is the fruit and these must co-exist. No society or nation can survive without a blend of the two. India and Thailand each have both aspects. The greatest bond between these countries is the blessing of Lord Buddha. He mentioned the 10 Paramitas: virtue in alms giving, morality, wisdom, perseverance, forbearance, truth friendliness. The Middle Path leads to peace and mental calm, which leads to nirvana. The Silk Route was a route of trade and exchange of ideas and the teaching of Buddha. In the present century though material wealth is increasing, peace and happiness are missing. Terrorism, violence, and modern problems are increasing. In this modern scenario, the middle path—Buddha's teaching/*dhamma*—is showing us the way.

S.M. Haldhar spoke of the relevance of Buddhism today in a paper entitled 'An Exploration of the Advent of Buddhism in Thailand'. He said that Thailand is an ancient nation and has always been politically independent. We should look at the relationship between all the Asian countries with special focus on Buddhism. There is a symbiotic relationship between the robe and the throne, ritual and temple power. We should explore the relationship that developed between Sri Lanka, Burma and Thailand. He spoke of the relationship between the monk and the kings; the Thai King is closely related to Buddhism; he must be a Buddhist, but must protect and support all religions.

Chirapat Prapandindya spoke on the 'Syncretism of Religions in Thailand'. His paper was based on inscriptions in Sanskrit, Khmer, and Pali languages up to the Ayutthiya period. He mentioned the Dvaravati period where the main objects for worship were the Buddha images, the Dharmachakra, and the stupa. He also referred to the Chenla kingdom whose Prince Chitrase erected Shivalingas and Nandi bulls throughout Thailand.

Bachchan Kumar spoke on 'Syncretism and Thai Buddhism'. He said that they grow together in a natural way. He dealt with related aspects of Buddhism, such as Theravada Buddhism and King Ramakhian and he presented slides from North Thailand as evidence.

Binay Kumar Mishra spoke on 'The Preserved Tradition of Mahayana in Thailand'. He said in his paper that so far Thailand is best studied by scholars from India.

SESSION 3: TAIS IN INDIA

The third session was moderated by Prof. Ravindra Panth. The first speaker, Wilawan Khanittanan discussed the Two Cultural Linkages

Between Thais and the Tais of India: Taoism and Buddhism. She divided her talk into two parts: (i) Buddhist background of Taoism and its cultural linkages, and (ii) the new linkage between Tais of India and Thailand. She brought in a Buddhist perspective and referred as well to Vietnam and Tai communities there.

J.N. Phukan spoke about the 'Tai Communities in India: Historical Background and Present State'. He said the Tais were microscopic communities in India and have been living there for several years in parts of Assam, Arunachal Pradesh, and Manipur. He spoke of six communities in Assam and Arunachal Pradesh—the Tai Ahom, Kantu, Phaket, Iton, Kaniyang, Turung which live in the river valley in low lying areas.

Ye Hom Buragohain, herself a Tai from Assam, spoke of how the Tai community in Assam lived. She stressed the social culture status and how Buddhism has been assimilated by the group in their lifestyle.

Prakong Ninmanahaminda gave a detailed report on the 'Tai Khamti of Arunachal Pradesh'. She described how much Buddhism dominates their culture and how they protect the words of the Buddha. They write the scriptures and store them in temples.

SESSION 4: THAI CULTURAL CENTRE

The fourth session was moderated by Dr. K.K. Basa. The first speaker, Srisurang Poothupya spoke of her experience with the Sunthanpoo Cultural Centre. She said that it may be more expensive to have a Centre in New Delhi but that 2007 was an appropriate time for its inauguration.

M.R. Chakrarot Chittrabongse gave a detailed account of his experience of setting up such centres. He mentioned that he is currently setting up the first Museum of the International Red Cross. He said that Buddhist temples as traditional cultural centres also function as community centres, and are places of learning and creative experience. They enable subsidiary functions like exhibitions, academic and learning.

Ravindra Panth suggested that the main centre be located in New Delhi with an extension branch elsewhere. He offered all his support if something was to be set up in Nalanda, Bihar.

Sachchidanand Sahai raised the important issue of how to keep the Cultural Centre specifically Thai.

CONCLUDING SESSION

In the concluding session, Satyavrat Shastri said that the Thais who have studied in India form a large number, and are a nucleus of the Indo-Thai relationship. He said that economic relations between the nations were improving, but language training was required for a better relationship. The Cultural Centre will fulfil all needs by showcasing Thailand to India. The Indians and Thais are not just friends. Ours is a symbiotic relationship.

Srisurang Poolthupya concluded by saying that Culture and Study Centres would help us to learn from each other directly. It is interesting to know how much Hindu scholars know about Buddhism. Our knowledge about Indian Art history would help us to know our Thai heritage.

Ravindra Kumar spoke about the Philosophy of Life and Practice of Buddhism in the Materialistic World of Modern Times. He enumerated the basic principles of Buddhism including *karuna* and its importance in attaining the final state or *nirvana.* He further added the necessity of following these principles in day to day life in order to attain freedom from sorrow.

Sachchidanand Sahai spoke on the relationship between the two countries that have been old, deep, and diverse. He referred to areas of possible study including the role of monarchy, the status and roles of monks, etc. He said the modern generation faces violence and tension and the words of the Buddha need to be revived again. One other area of study he mentioned was how the Thais and Thailand have contributed to the growth of Buddhism and the creation of a new Asian consciousness. He said that the Thai Dharamaputras are the parallel of the Thai Embassies around the world.

The papers presented at the seminar have been summarized above but it has not been possible to include the presentations and interventions of some scholars in this publication as the final version of their papers were not received till the time of going to the press. However, their vaulable contributions are gratefully acknowledged.

Message from Director General
Indian Council for Cultural Relations

I am happy that the Thai Embassy, New Delhi, and the Indian Council for Cultural Relations, New Delhi, have jointly organized a second seminar on Indo-Thai historical and cultural linkages. The first seminar, held in September 2005 in New Delhi, India, was the beginning of a stronger relationship between India and Thailand to further the age-old ties in the fields of language, religion, society, art and archaeology. These exchanges helped to highlight the unique cultures of the two countries as well as to extend the past associations to help form a new Asian presence in the world. This second seminar will be vital in extending the accomplishments of the first into newer avenues. These seminars will surely be important in forging a deeper and stronger bond between India and Thailand and I send my warmest wishes to the Thai people, the Indian Embassy in Bangkok, the organizers of the Seminar, and the participants.

PAVAN K. VARMA
Director General
Indian Council for Cultural Relations

Address by
H.E. Mr. Chirasak Thanesnant
Ambassador of Thailand

AT THE SECOND SEMINAR ON THAI-INDO HISTORICAL AND CULTURAL LINKAGES 21 AUGUST 2006

Your Excellency Mr. Deputy Permanent Secretary, Ministry of Foreign Affairs (Deputy Permanent Secretary Piyawat Niyomrerks), Mr. Thettalil Parameswaran P. Seetharam, Deputy Chief of Mission, the Embassy of India,
Distinguished speakers,
Ladies and gentlemen,

First of all, may I welcome the scholars from India to our City of Angels, Bangkok. It is indeed an honour and a privilege for me to be in the midst of such an imminent group of scholars. We are gathered here with one purpose in mind, and that is to foster the bilateral ties between Thailand and India, focusing on the historical and cultural aspects.

May I start by briefly informing you about the background of this seminar and its main objectives. The first seminar on Indo-Thai Historical and Cultural Linkages was held in New Delhi late last year, as a ground work for the establishment of a Thai Cultural Centre in India. The idea of establishing a Thai Cultural Centre in India was mutually agreed by the two Prime Ministers during the visit of Prime Minister Vajpayee to Thailand in 2004.

That seminar was successfully held with the collaboration of Indian Council for Cultural Relations. In my view, it was considered a success in many ways. Firstly, it was able to generate the interests of and positive response from scholars and participants alike in the proposed idea of establishing the Cultural Centre. Secondly, it was able to bring together prominent scholars from India and Thailand to discuss about the similarities in our culture, history, arts, linguistics, and ways to utilize these similarities. Lastly, the seminar was a beginning of a healthy relationship between the Royal Thai Embassy and ICCR, which I hope would continue to grow stronger in years to come.

Distinguished guests,
Ladies and Gentlemen,

As I mentioned earlier that the first seminar generated a high level of interest among participants about our plan to establish a Thai Cultural Centre, we therefore decided to make the seminar an annual event, which we would be holding in New Delhi and Bangkok alternately. This is to keep the momentum of the project and keep people involved, both Thai and Indian. Moreover, the meeting of Thai and Indian scholars on a regular basis would enhance the 'cultural diplomacy' between our two countries.

For the second seminar, here in Bangkok, we aim to explore how the historical and cultural linkages existing between Thailand and India for thousands of years, can be related to contemporary times and translated into tangible collaboration for the benefit of our peoples on the whole.

Ladies and Gentlemen,

I would like to stress that the most vital outcome that is expected from this seminar is a concrete plan for the establishment of the Thai Cultural Centre. We need a solid will from all concerned authorities in order to create a small move in the desired direction and eventually turn this project into reality.

Before I conclude, may I take this opportunity to thank the Deputy Permanent Secretary for sparing time out of his busy schedule to be with us. Also to Professor Sachchidanand Sahai and Assistant Professor Nongluk Thepsawasdi, Director of India Studies, whose advice was indispensable. I would also like to thank ICCR for the wonderful collaboration the Embassy has received all through this project. Most importantly, I would like to thank all the speakers and participants for their interest in making this seminar meaningful.

I wish the speakers and participants a fruitful deliberation and hope our bilateral relations are strengthened along the way. I look forward to welcoming you in India next year for our third seminar on Indo-Thai Historical and Cultural Linkages.

Thank you.

Philosophy of Life: Buddhism in Practice Today

RAVINDRA PANTH

Rare is the birth as a human being.
Hard is the life of mortals.
Hard is the hearing of the sublime truth (Dhamma).
Rare is the appearance of the Buddhas.[1]

It is indeed a gracious moment that we have all assembled here today to participate in this seminar in Bangkok. The event becomes all the more important as this is the auspicious 2550th Mahaparinirvana Jayanti of Lord Buddha being celebrated throughout India.

It is rightly said that history and culture are interdependent. They cannot exist and prosper in isolation. Metaphorically speaking, they are two essential parts of a tree—history is the root and culture the fruit. Culture without history has no root, whereas history without culture bears no fruit. A nation is like a tree. If it has no history, it will never survive and grow in totality, and if it has no culture, it will never develop and progress in a holistic way. A nation with history and culture alone is a long-living and flourishing tree that can weather any storm and withstand any climate. India and Thailand have historic and cultural links and this conference will fulfil its aim of strengthening the eternal friendship and cooperation between the two countries.

The greatest bond of mutual friendship and cooperation between our countries since ancient times was laid by the Enlightened One and for that both countries must pay respect to Lord Buddha, the Great Master, who showed, preached, and taught to suffering humanity the Middle Path of Peace, Harmony, and Happiness. This path is universal in character, and is based on *sīla* (morality), *samādhi* (concentration) and *paññā* (wisdom). On this occasion we should not merely remember Lord Buddha but should practise his teachings in our daily life; then alone will we pay him true respect, and gain from his Dhamma.

If we glance through his early life, the tradition says, Siddhartha as Bodhisattva, that is, Buddha in becoming, himself practised the ten *Pāramitās* or virtues towards perfection. These virtues or qualities are: virtue in alms giving (*dāna-pāramī*), morality (*sīla-pāramī*), renunciation (*nekhamma-pāramī*), wisdom (*paññā-pāramī*), perseverance (*viriya-pāramī*), forbearance (*khanti-pāramī*), truthfulness (*sacca-pāramī*), determination (*adhitthāna-pāramī*), friendliness (*mettā-pāramī*), and equanimity (*upekkhā-pāramī*).

These ten *pāramitās* are nothing but set of human values or qualities that nature has given us as a human being to develop, which Siddhartha Gautama also practised and perfected and thus attained Perfect Enlightenment on the full moon day of Vesakha under the tree now revered by all as *Bodhi*, in Bodh Gaya. It was on the same full moon day that Siddhartha Gautama was born in Lumbini, and also the same day of Vesakha full moon day when at the ripe age of eighty he passed into *Mahāparinirvāna* at Kushinagar.

At this occassion I am reminded of his first sermon to the five mendicants (*pañca vaggiya bhikkhūs*) who became his disciples at Sarnath, where he mentioned the essence of his teaching: the Eightfold Path or Middle Path (*majjhima patipada*). The Enlightened One said:

> Monks, those who are in search of Truth must always avoid the two extremes. The first extreme to be avoided is the life of ease and luxury, as it enslaves man to gross needs and debases his human qualities. The second is the life of self torture through penance, because it is not only painful, but useless. The Middle Path is the best: it produces insight and mental calm, which ultimately lead to Nirvana.
>
> And what is the Middle Path? It is a state of self-discipline, through an eightfold endeavour. I call it the eightfold path—consisting of right understanding, right aspiration, right speech, right conduct, right livelihood, right effort, right mindfulness and right concentration. One who follows this eightfold path develops an insight and a mental calm which ultimately lead to Nirvana.[2]

Lord Buddha was a visionary. Out of compassion for mankind, he started his mission soon after his Enlightenment, and advised his disciples too to do the same. 'Go forth, O! Monks for the good of many for the happiness of many, out of compassion for the world, for the good, benefit and happiness of god and men.'

It was mainly because of its universal teaching that Buddhism has been successful at various times in its history. It was because of this that it enjoyed the royal patronage of kings and dynasties in the time of Buddha, and also later, and even today. Similarly people of all walks of society have accepted Buddhism whether in the business community or among intellectuals or the commoners and downtrodden. The Silk Route of ancient times is witness to the tremendous volume of trade that existed in the ancient world, which was also a route for exchange and spread of ideas and teachings of Buddha as well. Due to its universal principles and scientific base even in the modern time, the teaching of Buddha has reached out to people in society at large.

As we know, the twentieth century has been the forerunner of materialistic developments in a broad range of human activities in economic, social, politics and science and technology, etc. On the one hand mankind had made tremendous material progress but the blue bird of happiness is still eluding us. There is utter poverty, conflict and mass abuse of the earth's resources all around. Different types of violence and terrorism are increasing. Problems of racial discrimination, the repression of ethnic and religious minorities, and the denial of equal rights are increasing day by day. There is an environment of corruption and dishonesty, hatred and indifference towards others. It is a proven fact that the weakening of human values and equalities has caused serious social problems.

Under these circumstances, the Middle Path of Buddha, with its principles of love, friendliness, non-violence, moderation, mutual cooperation and co-existence have become paramount in importance. Every individual in society is seeking a solution to the problems of materialism: greed, jealousy, hatred, poverty, conflict, and suffering. Lord Buddha, like a skilled physician, is able to provide medicine in the form of his Dhamma (teaching).

According to Buddhism, human values arise in the human mind and should be well cultivated. How? Lord Buddha says :

> Not to do any evil, to cultivate good,
> To purify one's mind—this is the Teaching of the Buddhas. . . .

Forbearing patience is the highest austerity, Nirvana is supreme, say the Buddhas,
He is not a recluse who harms another, nor is he an ascetic who oppresses others.
Not insulting, not harming, restraint according to the Fundamental Moral Code.
Moderation in food, secluded abode, intent on higher thoughts –
This is the Teaching of the Buddhas.[3]

The mind is the root cause of all human activities, whether good or bad. If one can remove all evil thoughts from the mind, one can attain a happy and peaceful life. To attain peaceful life one should be involved in good thoughts and good activities by practising forbearance and patience and by not insulting or harming others. The Buddha always emphasized right action and the purification of one's mind, living a pure, happy, and harmonious life. The basic purpose of his teachings is to expound a way of life to be followed and practised by each individual. When practised, I am sure Buddhism with its basic path can eradicate social upheaval and remove extremes like terrorism and violence.

The Buddha was a practical thinker. He advised the seeker not to accept anything merely on the authority of another but to exercise his own reasoning and judge for himself whether a thing is right or wrong. He gave to the world the freedom to think. He did not put forward a set of dogmas. What he taught was verifiable. His advise to Kalamas stands as a charter of intellectual freedom, the first exposition of pragmatism.

Do not accept anything on mere hearsay. Do not accept anything by mere tradition (i.e., thinking that it has thus been handed down through many generations). Do not accept anything on account of rumors (i.e., by believing what others say without any investigation). Do not accept anything just because it accords with your scriptures. Do not accept anything by mere supposition. Do not accept anything by mere inference. Do not accept anything by merely considering the appearances. Do not accept anything merely because it agrees with your preconceived notions. Do not accept anything merely because it seems acceptable (i.e., should be accepted). Do not accept anything thinking that the ascetic is respected by us (and, therefore, it is right to accept his word).

But when you know for yourselves—these things are immoral, these things are blameworthy, these things are censured by the wise, these things, when performed and undertaken, conduce to ruin and sorrow—then indeed do you reject them.

When you know for yourselves—these things are moral, these things are blameless, these things are praised by the wise, these things, when performed and undertaken, conduce to well-being and happiness—then do you live and act accordingly.[4]

Buddhist teaching has nothing secret, no hidden meanings. It invites scrutiny and reasoned criticism. Again, in the *Jñanasāra Samuccaya* Buddha states, 'As the wise test gold by burning, cutting and examining by means of a touchstone, so should you accept any words after examining them and not merely out of regard and reverence of me'. He also taught people to allow freedom of worship. 'If others speak against me or my religion, that is no reason why you should be angry. If you do so, you will not know, if what they say is true or false.'[5] Tolerance does not mean that one should hide the light of truth from another. The Dhamma should be taught out of goodwill and compassion, and never with bitterness.

Freedom to live is another important feature of this teaching and is relevant in today's society. Every living being is attached to its life and dreads pain and suffering. Besides this universality, as of suffering. He taught of many others. One such was the brotherhood among all beings and not of men only. One cannot say how beings have been related to one another in past lives as parents, brothers, sisters, or friends. So every one should live in harmony with each other as we are interconnected with each other in same way or the other in this world.

Buddha's disapproval of class distinctions in contemporary caste-ridden India was revolutionary. He declared: 'Not by birth does a person become an outcaste, not by birth does one become a Brahman. But by deeds one becomes an out-caste and by deeds one becomes a Brahman.'[6] To his Order of Monks, nobles and out-castes were admitted without discrimination and they lived the pure life without pernicious views of high and low.

The Buddha was a great scientist, his contribution was to rescue man from dependence on the concept of god and divine law for his salvation. In so doing he taught self-help, self-knowledge, and self-reverence (the word 'self' is used only as a mode of speech). He says, 'Ye yourselves must walk the path, Buddhas merely teach the way.'[7] In man lay vast undeveloped powers for the attainment of which he has to strive. His frequent exhortation was, 'Abide with the Dhamma as an islands, with the Dhamma as a refuge. Seek not another refuge'.[8]

The contribution of Buddha to the world is a profound analysis of and a practical solution for the problem of human suffering. Much of his legacy is in giving importance to his teachings in the different scriptures as per the need of the people.

Right from early history, we know that spread of Buddhism from the land of its birth was not at the cost of bloodshed but as an encompassing philosophy of universal love, non-violence, and compassion. At the time of its dissemination Buddhism had assimilated the nature, faith, and practices from the place where it had reached.

Respect for the cultures, civilizations, and religions of each other, and no interference or conversion by a subtle psychological agenda, should be the values of humankind in our century. To maintain harmony in the states, the Buddha has suggested some seven principles they are propounded in the last discourse called the *Mahaparinibbana Sutta*. I conclude my paper with it.

> So long as the princes assemble in harmony, disperse in harmony, and carry out their business in harmony and act in accordance with the ancient institutions of the Vajjians and they honour and esteem and revere and support the elders and follow their words, and refraining from forcibly abducting and detaining the women and girls they should be treated with utmost care and honour. So long as they esteem honour and revere their shrines within and without the city and cause appropriate offerings and oblations to be made to those shrines as formally without negligence or omission. So long as they take appropriate measures to afford proper care, protection and security to the *arhats* so that they may enter and live at ease and comfort, so that by following these suggestion the furtherance of their welfare and prosperity is to be expected not their decline.[9]

NOTES

1. *Dhammapada*, Verse 182.
2. *Dhammacakkappavattana Sutta*, *Mahavaggapali*, *Vinayapitaka*.
3. *Dhammapada*, Verse 183-5.
4. *Kesamutti Suttam*, *Anguttaranikaya*.

5. *Brahmajala Sutta, Dighanikaya.*
6. *Vasala Suttam*, Verse 142, *Suttanipata.*
7. *Dhammapada*, Verse 176.
8. *Mahaparinibbana Sutta, Dighanikaya.*
9. Ibid.

Celebrating the Indo-Thai Cultural Heritage: Some Issues and Challenges for the Thai Cultural Centre

KISHOR K. BASA

We are not only at the beginning of a new millennium, but also in a period of transition. The complexities of our time have been addressed in various ways. While Touraine considers it the 'end of industrial society', Lash and Urry perceive it as the 'end of organized capitalism'. Globalization, that has emerged as an ideology and currently dominates our thinking, policy-making, and political practice is the major problem before us. It is well known that the globalization project 'benefits the rich', since forms of equality within actual inequality are favourable to the dominant. Accepting that in the public domain globalization is considered as 'economically benign' and 'socially malign', Bhagwati argued that globalization is good but needs appropriate governance.

There are sharply contradictory views as regards the relationship between globalization and culture. While Bhagwati stated that economic globalization is 'culturally enriching process', involving hybridization, Kapur argued that what is being globalized is the American style of capitalism and its implicit world-view. Raising the issues to a more complex level, Appadurai argued that while the formats in which meanings are being expressed might be increasingly similar, they are differentially appropriated depending on the needs and creative dimensions of indigenous people. Stating that we are functioning in a world fundamentally characterized by objects in motion, Appadurai emphasized the 'non-isomorphic' nature of global cultural flows, which, according to him, are of five kinds: ethnoscape, mediascape, technoscape, financescape and ideoscape. He did not subscribe to the view that culture merely flows from 'global centre' to 'subordinate peripheries'; rather, cultural innovation in the centre is also brought in by the so-called periphery. Another debatable issue is a sharply divided opinion as to whether globalization would lead to the withering away of the nation state. Whatever be the consequence, identity construction has emerged as an important issue either as a response to the threat of cultural homogenization or as a means of celebrating diversity.

With this general background, we may discuss issues relevant to the Thai Cultural Centre in India. The discussion falls under the following head: the antiquity of Indo-Thai trade and exchange, Intangible Cultural Heritage, the implications of heritage for tourism, and issues in museology and archaeology.

ANTIQUITY OF INDO-THAI TRADE AND EXCHANGE

The antiquity of Indo-Thai cultural relations may be traced to the Neolithic period (around the second millennium BC) characterized by the movement of Austro-Asiatic linguistic groups to north-east India from an area comprising south China and northern mainland South-East Asia including Thailand. While prehistorians would argue the occurrence of the shouldered adze/axe and cord-impressed pottery as material evidence of such interaction, physical anthropologists have emphasized the presence of Haemoglobin E among some of the populations of north-eastern India as a result of this movement and interaction.

However, the earliest evidence of maritime contact between India and Thailand is known from the Iron Age site of Ban Don Ta Phet in the Kanchanaburi Province, west-central Thailand, dated to about 350 BC (Fig. 1). The archaeological evidence for early Indo-Thai maritime trade and exchange comprises glass beads, etched agate and carnelian beads, knobbed vessels and high-tin bronze artefacts (Fig. 2).

Glass Beads

Monochrome glass beads of different colours, best known collectively as Indo-Pacific glass beads, are the most common bead type in late prehistoric South-East Asia. Among them, opaque brown-red and orange-red *mutisalah* beads constitute an important class.

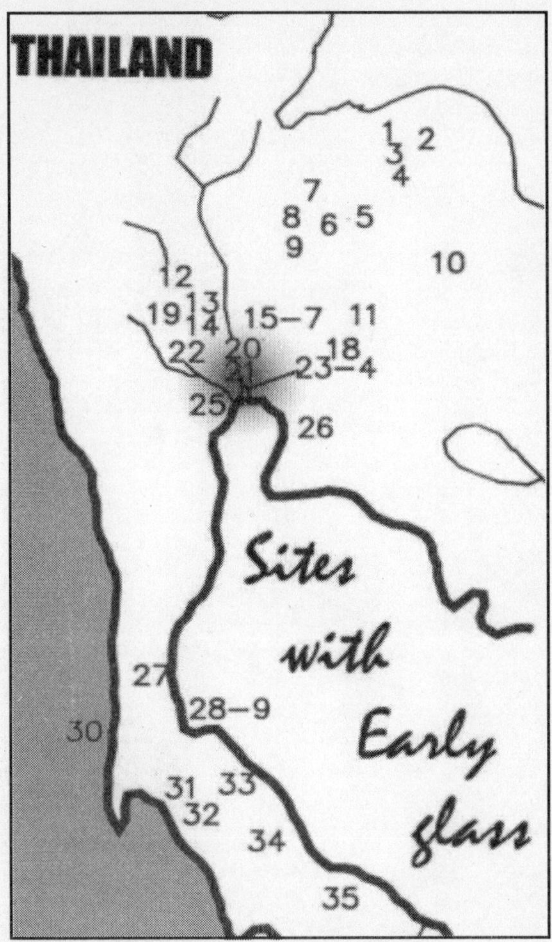

Fig. 1: Sites with Early Glass

In South Asia, the earliest evidence of red glass beads comes from Rajghat from Period IB (*c.* 600–500 BC) and from the Bhir Mound, Taxila (*c.* fifth century BC). Arikamedu on the coast of south India was one of the most important manufacturing centres of monochrome glass beads including the opaque brown-red *mutisalah* varieties (Fig. 3). In Thailand, they have been found in many late prehistoric sites such as Ban Chiang (Fig. 4), Ban Na Di, Non Muang, Ban Tha Kae, Ban Don Ta Phet (Fig. 5), Prasat Muang Sing and Kok Ra Ka.

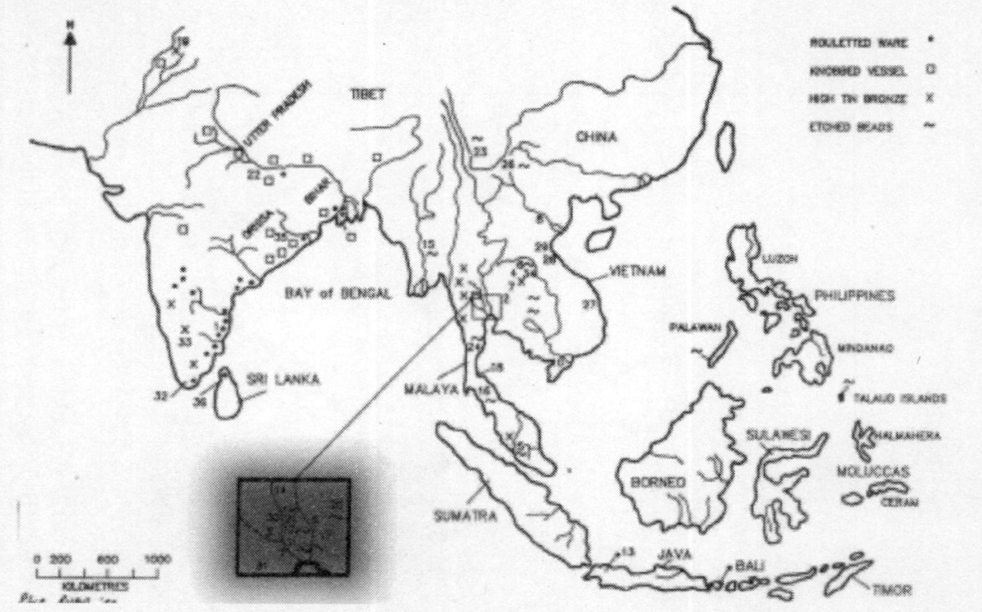

Key to the numbered sites: 1 Arikamedu, 2 Kok Charoen, 3 Ban Kao, 4 Ban Na Di, 5 Tha Khae, 6 Ban Chiang, 7 Non Nok Tha, 8 Phung Nguyen, 9 Pong Tuk, 10 Oc-eo, 11 Ban Don Ta Phet, 12 U-Thong, 13 Buni, 14 Chansen, 15 Beikthano, 16 Khlong Thom, 17 Saraburi, 18 Chaiya, 19 Taxila, 20 Khao Mogul, 21 Ban Plai Nam, 22 Bhita, 23 Likiang, 24 Khao Sam Kao, 25 Kuala Selinsing, 26 Shi Zhai Shan & Lijiashan, 27 Sa Huynh, 28 Xuan An, 29 Dongson, 30 Tham Ongbah, 31 Chombung, 32 Adittanalur, 33 Coimbatome, 34 Kok Khon, 35 Sisulpalgarh, 36 Mantai.

Fig. 2: Distribution of etched beads, knobbed vessles, high-tin bronze and rouletted ware in India and South-East Asia (from Glover 1989).

Fig. 3: Arikamedu: Monochrome drawn glass beads.

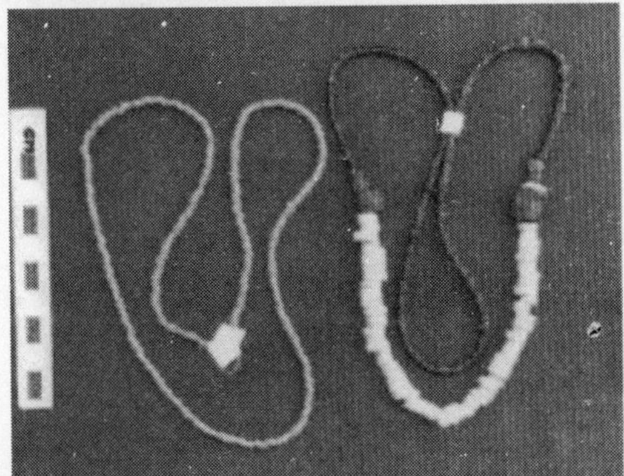

Fig. 4: Ban Chiang: Monochrome glass beads.

The earliest evidence for the manufacture of glass beads in Thailand comes from Khlong Thom, dated from about the fourth century onwards. Thus it is reasonable to infer that most, if not all, of the monochrome glass beads were imported from India. The opaque *mutisalah* beads, especially, I think, would have come primarily from south India.

A type of opaque black round bead with spiral grooves is found at Prasat Muang Sing (Fig. 6) in Thailand. It appears that the spiral grooves were originally filled with white strips. A similar bead was found at Ban Chi Nam Lai, Inburi district, Singhburi province, from

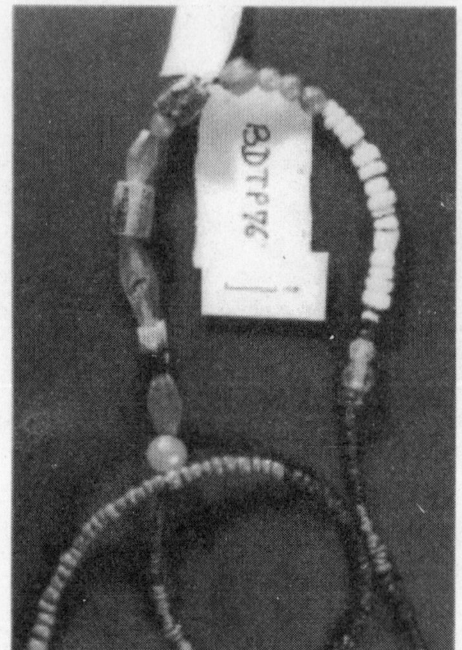

Fig. 5: Ban Don Ta Phet: Monochrome beads.

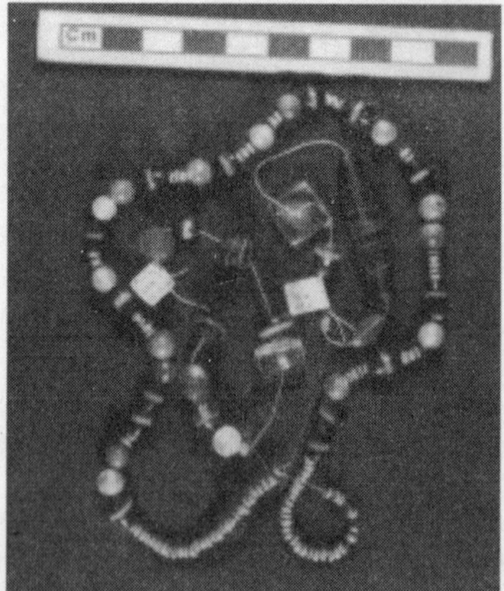

Fig. 6: Prasat Muang Sing beads.

Fig. 7: Narhan: Glass beads and a bangle piece. Bottom left: hexagonal barrel; bottom middle: hexagonal biconical; top right: black bead with white spiral strip.

the surface collection. Rare in South-East Asia, this is a typical north Indian bead, and has been found in surface collections from Kausambi and the excavations at Narhan, Chandraketugarh, and Kodumanal. At Kodumanal it is dated *c*. 100 BC–AD 200. At Narhan in eastern Uttar Pradesh, it is dated to the Gupta period (Fig. 7).

Ban Chiang and Ban Don Ta Phet have also yielded translucent clear greenish hexagonal prisms, hexagonal barrels, square prisms, and square barrels (Fig. 8). For Glover, from the point of view of trade with India, the most interesting glass bead is the large hexagonal prism, similar to the beryl crystals of south India which were very popular in Buddhist cultures of north India and in the Roman world (they caught the attention of Pliny the Elder). According to Francis, hexagonal prisms closely imitating beryl (which Pliny mentioned) were manufactured at Arikamedu. In my 1988 study of glass beads, I saw only a few similar beads in surface collections from Ahichhatra

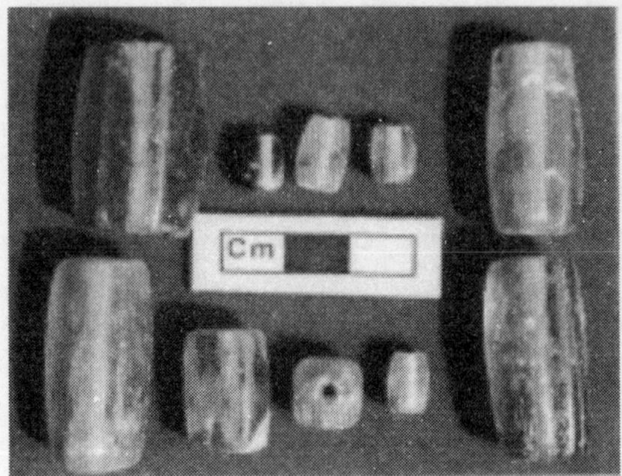

Fig. 8: Ban Don Ta Phet: Prismatic glass beads (including barrels).

and Kausambi (Fig. 9) in the Allahabad Museum, and a hexagonal barrel type from Narhan. The latter is dated to 290 ± 100 BC, 250 ± 100 BC and 150 ± 100 BC. Two hexagonal barrels of almost

Fig. 9: Kausambi glass beads (see hexagonal barrel bead in the middle).

colourless glass are also documented from the Bhir Mound, Taxila (Pakistan) of the fourth-third century BC.

With regard to their chemical composition, the analysis of twenty-four glass beads—eighteen from Ban Don Ta Phet, one from Ban Chiang in Thailand and five from Sembiran (Bali) in Indonesia—shows that the glass can be divided into two main types, mixed-alkali glass and potassium glass. All the six mixed-alkali glass beads analysed had soda as the main alkali, along with relatively high alumina (< 3.5 per cent) and low lime (< 5 per cent)—the two most important characteristics of Indian glass. Eighteen glass beads have potassium oxide as their main alkali, although in most cases a little soda is also present. Of these, thirteen are from Ban Don Ta Phet, one from Ban Chiang, and four from Sembiran. Both Han China and India have yielded potassium-rich glass. The import of potassium glass from China to Ban Don Ta Phet in the late centuries BC seems unlikely since the forms of early Thai beads closely resemble those of India, and there is no other evidence of Chinese material on the site.

However, it must be stated that not all sources for the many kinds of glass have been fully determined. For example, to my knowledge, there is as yet no parallel to the tubular glass beads with oblique cut ends, obtained from the surface collection from Ban Chiang (Fig. 10). Except at Oc Eo in Vietnam, the bipyramidal glass beads from Ban Don Ta Phet do not have any parallel either.

Fig. 10: Ban Chiang glass: left to right – ear ornament, hexagonal barrel bead and obliquely truncated tubular beads.

Etched agate and carnelian beads

The best evidence of trade in semi-precious stone beads between South and South-East Asia lies in the etched agate and etched carnelian beads. The technique of etching involves the use of a paste of natural soda and crushed shoots of the *kirar* plant (*Capparis aphylla*) which is applied before the stone bead is baked. Beck discussed etched beads under three periods, of which Period II, dated between 300 BC–AD 200, is relevant to us. More than 50 etched beads were found in Ban Don Ta Phet (Fig. 11). Etched beads are also reported from Ban Chiang, U-Thong, Krabi, and Khao Sam Kao in Thailand. Most of these beads belong to Type 1 of Beck. On them a white design is etched on the polished stone surface of natural red or grayish black colour. As for Ban Don Ta Phet, Glover pointed out that a closer match to the etched beads comes from Uttar Pradesh and Bihar and Taxila.

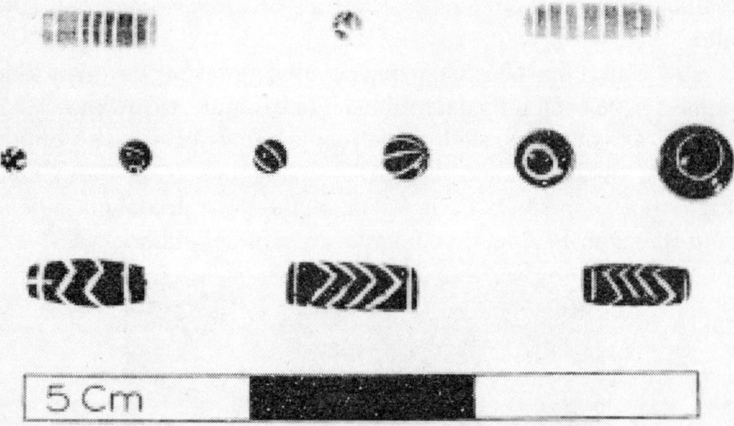

Fig. 11: Etched beads from Ban Don Ta Phet (from Glover 1989).

Knobbed Vessels

Glover emphasized the significance of the knobbed-base vessels from Thailand (Fig. 12) and India and argued that they were associated with Buddhist rituals. About 20–30 bronze bowls from Ban Don Ta Phet have a conical boss, sometimes cast integral to the vessel but often made separately and riveted through a hole in the

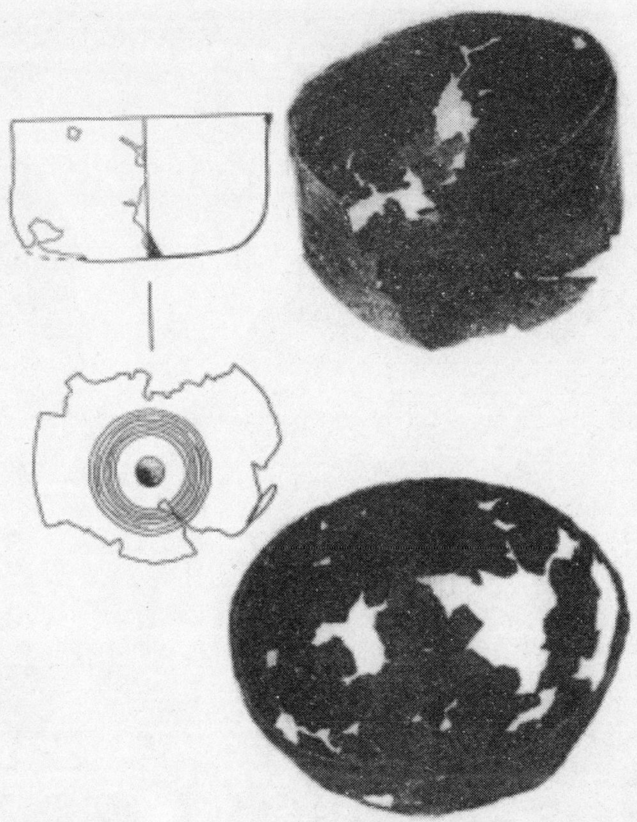

Fig. 12: Knobbed-base, high-tin cast bronze vessels from Ban Don Ta Phet (from Glover 1989).

base. The conical boss is surrounded by incised circles, often seven. Parallels for this vessel type are known in a modified form in South Asia in the form of high tin bronze bowls from the Nilgiris, a silver dish from Taxila, and a splendid granite bowl from Taxila. This is also replicated in a pottery form known as 'knobbed-ware' in India, reported for the first time at Sisupalgarh in Orissa (Fig. 13) in 1949, and recovered primarily on the north Andhra, Orissa, and Bengal coasts and dated to late centuries BC. The precise function of these vessels is not known, but Glover argued that they were not meant for any utilitarian purpose. The knob and circles perhaps implied a *mandala*.

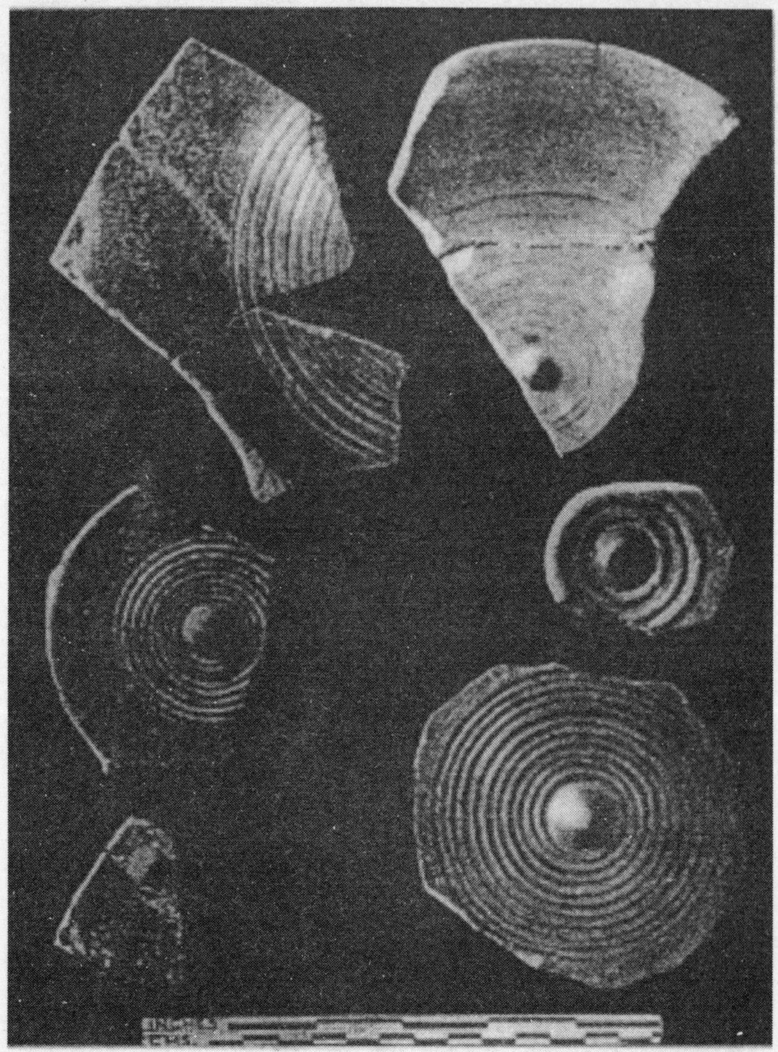

Fig. 13: Knobbed ware pottery from Sisupalgarh (from Lal 1949).

High-tin Bronze

Bronze vessels with a very high tin content (23–28 per cent), cast with thin walls and manufactured by hot working, quenching, and annealing were reported from Ban Don Ta Phet. Despite their brittleness, these bowls are thought to have been valued for their yellow, gold-like colour when freshly polished. In Thailand, such artefacts are also reported at Kok Khon in Sakorn Nakorn Province, from the late prehistoric Iron Age levels at Ban Chiang and Ban Na Di in north-east Thailand, from Tham Ongbah on the Kwae Yai river in western Thailand, and from Khao Jamook, Suen Peung district, west of Rajburi. Rajpitak and Seeley mention the sporadic recovery of high-tin bronze at Adichanallur in Tinnevelly district, at Coimbatore, and at Taxila. Copper-tin artefacts are rare in India which is deficient in tin and not too brittle brass items were just coming into use. Hence, it has been argued that the high-tin, cast bronze vessels were imported from Thailand, partly because of its gold-like colour. However, recently Sarada Srinivasan has drawn our attention to a living tradition of high-tin bronze making in south India.

Thus, the antiquity of the Indo-Thai maritime contact can be traced back to the fourth century BC on the basis of excavations at Ban Don Ta Phet. Two things may be mentioned here. Citing the opaque black bead with the spiral white strips, it could be argued that the tiny glass bead has the potential to tell a story of its use and trade, as well as a route from the western Ganga valley to Bengal and then Thailand. Second, two carnelian lion pendants—recovered from Ban Don Ta Phet (Fig. 14a, 14b)—might imply *sakyasimha*, the lion of the Sakya clan. In the Jatakas, it is held, when the people gathered together and 'took for their king a certain man, handsome, auspicious, commanding, altogether perfect, the quadrupeds also gathered and chose for their king the Lion' (Tambiah 1976).

INTANGIBLE CULTURAL HERITAGE

Heritage has been described by Germaine Greer as the 'cultural expression of what makes us what we are, our spiritual DNA'. Intangible Cultural Heritage (ICH) is usually associated with traditional knowledge systems. According to the UNESCO Convention of October 2003 it means the 'practices, representations, expressions, knowledge, skills—as well as the instruments, objects, artefacts and cultural spaces associated therewith—that communities, groups and, in some cases, individuals recognize as part of

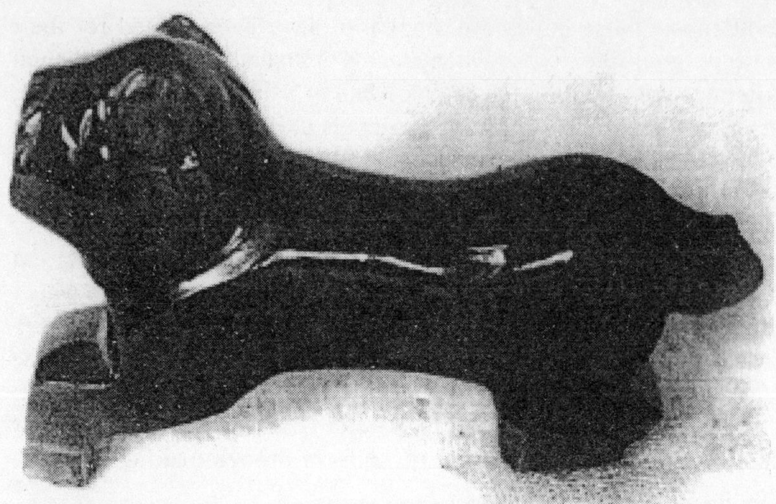

Fig. 14a: Carnelian leaping lion pendant from Ban Don Ta Phet (from Glover 1989).

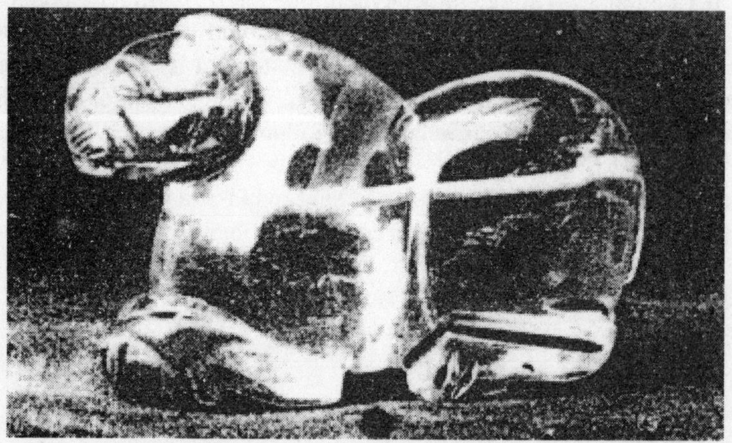

Fig. 14b: Crystal crouched lion pendant from the Dharmarajika stupa, Taxila (from Marshall 1951).

their cultural heritage'. Sometimes called living cultural heritage, this is manifested in the following domains: 'oral traditions, expression and languages; the performing arts; social practices, rituals and festive events; knowledge and practices about nature and the universe; and traditional craftsmanship'. ICH is subjected to constant collective recreation by communities and groups in response to environment, interaction with nature, and the historical conditions of existence. A sense of identity and continuity is thereby fostered. Last but not the least, its safeguarding 'promotes, sustains and develops cultural diversity and human creativity'. Cultural diversity, according to the Universal Declaration of UNESCO, is 'one of the roots of development' and 'as necessary for humankind as is biodiversity for nature'.

Some staggering facts have been provided by UNESCO in relation to endangered languages which call for collective action for documentation, preserving, promoting and disseminating ICH. It has been stated, for example, that '(1) 90 per cent of the world's languages are not represented on the internet; (2) one language is disappearing on average every two weeks; (3) 80 per cent of African languages lack orthographies; (4) half of the all languages occur in just eight countries: Papua New Guinea (832), Indonesia (731), Nigeria (515), India (400), Mexico (295), Cameroon (286), Australia (268), and Brazil (234)'. There is a steady threat to such languages in these countries. Let us now discuss some activities of our museum which have relevance for Thailand.

Work of IGRMS (Bhopal) on ICH relevant to Thailand

The distinction between the tangible and intangible, in a way, is a heuristic device since a tangible heritage might have an intangible dimension and vice versa. Therefore a comprehensive heritage study must not segregate, but must encompass both the categories. Keeping this in view, the example of two projects of IGRMS are cited here.

The first project involves documentation of the World Heritage Site of Bhimbetka undertaken by our Museum, emphasizing the various ethnic groups such as Daroi Gond, Korku, and Bhilala, with regard to their life cycle rituals, arts and crafts, folk tales and myths and other aspects of traditional knowledge system. I hasten to add here that the methods and strategies for undertaking such study on ICH vary from site to site. Keeping this in view, we are planning to study two more World Heritage Sites, Hampi and Konark in the near future. Such studies around heritage sites and monuments have great potential in Thailand too. This could lead to a comprehensive understanding of heritage as whole.

The second project involves the Sacred Groves of India. Sacred Groves are the 'Gardens of Gods', consisting of natural vegetation of the locality, and the associated supernatural power. In India, sacred groves are known under different names, *Deorais* or *Devrahati* in Maharashtra, *Sarna* or *Dev* in Jharkhand and Chhatisgarh, *Oran* in Rajasthan, *Sidharavana* or *Devara-kodu* or *Pavitravana* in Karnataka, *Kovil-Kadu* or *Thiru-nanda-vana* in Tamil Nadu and *Pavitravana* or *Kavu* in Kerala. Following serious depletion and mismanagement of living resources by the modern industrialized societies, there arose, in the recent past, a new interest among ecologists to revive community-organized systems of ecological conversation. Their prospects depend largely on effective community participation. In 1999, IGRMS installed on its 200-acre campus at Bhopal, replicas of sacred groves from Kerala, Tamil Nadu, Meghalaya, Jharkhand, Chhatisgarh, Rajasthan and Maharashtra. These were ritually established by dance and ceremonies performed by the respective communities. Plants from groups of these states were planted in their respective replicas after very careful selection, taking into consideration the geoclimatic condition of Bhopal. After concluding a festival on sacred groves and an outdoor exhibition at IGRMS, the participants felt that this precious collection needs to be taken to rural communities, with a view to providing them with information about sacred groves in different parts of the country. Therefore, IGRMS developed a travelling exhibition. The aim of this exhibition is (1) to interact with local organizations and people to learn more about sacred groves of the country and (2) to strengthen the variety of sacred groves related to local management practices and knowledge system. The Thai Cultural Centre could play a crucial role in networking relevant institutions and organizations in India and Thailand.

The Intangible Cultural Heritage of Indian Communities of Tai Origin

An important component of ICH of India is such a study on the communities of Tai origin. A case study of the Khamtis of north-east India may provide a good example. In the social hierarchy of Tai Buddhist migrants, the Khamtis occupy the highest position. The word Khampti means 'a land full of gold'. A Buddhist tribe, the

Khamtis mainly live in Lohit district of Arunachal Pradesh. They are also found in the Tirap district of Arunachal Pradesh as well as in the districts of Dibrugarh and Lakhimpur of Assam. Khamti houses are strong timber structures with raised floors and thatched roofs. Floors are made of bamboo. Every Khamti village has a vihara, called *Kyong* or *Chong*. Dalton writes, 'The temple and priests' quarter are also of timber and thatched, but the temples are elaborately carved, and great neatness and taste are evinced in the arrangement of the internal fittings.' The public granary is an important feature of the Khamti village, usually constructed near a water source. The method of construction of house, vihara, and granary, as well as various rituals associated in the making of the structures, are aspects of ICH. The community has its own script and the people speak in Khamti which belongs to the Tai family of language. A documentation of their myths, legends, and stories, is also the need of the hour. The Khamtis belong to the Hinayana sect, but their religion is tinged with traditional beliefs and practices. They believe in family, village and clan spirits. Documentation of these activities is also important. Audio-visual documentation of the various festivals would also be useful. Such documentation is also necessary for textile production, wood-carving, idol-making and basket-making, as well as for traditional songs and dances.

TOURISM

Globalization, both of economy and information system, has accelerated the processes of tourism, travel, and migration. It has been claimed that tourism is becoming the biggest industry in the world in 'a global village' and the life blood of much of that industry is heritage (Boniface and Fowler 1993: Preface). Kelleher (2004) points out an interesting dimension of heritage tourism. While people seeking heritage tourism desire authenticity of place and experience, the growth and profitability of heritage tourism has resulted in a proliferation of inauthenticity. As the number of contrived historical displays increases, inauthentic historical material becomes more deeply embedded in 'our' culture. Kelleher refers to Eric Cohen's explanation of this phenomenon as one in which 'contrived attractions, originally created for tourist purposes, increasingly become part of the physical, historical or cultural environment—

they become naturalized'. This blurs the distinction between 'natural' and 'contrived' attractions. For some, the impact of tourism has been claimed to be devastating at a cultural level. For example, speaking about its impact on the Haitian culture, Louis Turner and John Ash argued in the 1970s that 'tourism is, everywhere the enemy of authenticity and cultural identity'. Even in a developed country like France, the setting up of Euro Disneyland led some of the Paris intelligentsia to describe the new site as a 'cultural Chernobyl' (Boniface and Fowler 1993:148). Speaking about India, Singh (2000: 61) stated that tourism poses problems of cultural intrusion on the local cultures in selected high intensity tourist spots in Rajasthan, Goa, Uttar Pradesh and Karnataka.

However, in the face of globalization in the economy and the desire to earn hard currency as a means of propping up the domestic economy, tourism is considered an important way out. In this regard, infrastructure near important heritage sites would be/are being developed or various theme parks would be set up. In India emphasis on heritage tourism is known by the stress given, for example, to monuments in Delhi, Agra (Taj Mahal), Rajasthan (forts and palaces), Ajanta and Ellora in central India, Mahabalipuram near Chennai (Madras) and Thanjavur, and the Golden Triangle of coastal Orissa. Partly to promote tourism, cultural festivals are organized near heritage sites. In a way this shows an applied dimension of heritage studies. In order to attract tourists, some new trends have developed in museums. For example one now finds displays about different ethnic groups, their houses and their material culture in traditional surroundings, as is the case with 'mini Indonesia' near Jakarta. Sometimes 'craft villages' are displayed, such as the village near Puri in coastal Orissa.

Pilgrimage is the old mode of tourism. The Thai Cultural Centre should help in networking such tourism between India and Thailand. However, while developing ethnic tourism, attempts should be made to emphasize both continuity and change, rather than romanticize the ethnic group as if they are part of the cabinet of colonial curiosity. Visits to Buddhist sites in India have also important bearing. Archaeological sites and monuments in Thailand showing cultural relations between India and Thailand would be attractive for Indian tourists in Thailand. However, in the interpretation centres, the uniqueness of Thai traditions and the Thai element in the incorporation of ideas and artefacts from India should be emphasized to demonstrate that, even in antiquity, Thailand played an active agent of social process rather than being a passive recipient.

ISSUES IN MUSEOLOGY AND ARCHAEOLOGY

While on the one hand there has been an increase in the number of museums globally, on the other hand, the trend does not necessarily 'indicate security' since some trends in museums question the authenticity and grand narratives of the nation state, diversifying the form and content. For example, some museums tackle controversial subjects in controversial ways: the Holocaust Memorial Museum in Washington D.C., the Museum of Famine, Ireland are examples. In some other cases, museums are being appropriated to other cultural idioms. In Australia, in some exhibitions on the aboriginals, instead of having a White view of aboriginal history and archaeology, both the aboriginal and White views are included. Moreover, New Museology and Eco-Museology have become important trends in the museum movement, where people are treated as the curators of heritage and the role of the museologist is that of a facilitator. While 'culture' has been the key concept in anthropological museums all through, a major challenge anthropological museums encounter is how to reconcile the celebration of cultural identities of all possible forms and the potential threat some of them pose to the concept of the contemporary nation state. Another corollary is how to display the diaspora in an age when non-resident Indians are playing an increasingly important role in our economy and culture than hitherto. Locating the subtle and creative dimension of global-local relationships and displaying it in museums is another challenge for anthropological museums.

In archaeology the ascendance of globalization has implications for using archaeological sites (including the World Heritage Sites) for tourism and diaspora studies. But globalization has not necessarily resulted in the withering away of nationalism. On the other hand, nationalism has emerged as an important issue in contemporary archaeology. Besides, 'the unreflective Euro-centric view', of museum display in archaeological museums where a particular 'frozen' moment in time is captured as if it is perennial, is being questioned. Moreover, there are issues of trafficking of antiquities from the Third World, and the problems of their repatriation. To address such issues, separate workshops on museology and archaeology could be held by scholars of Thailand and India. Moreover, a few exhibitions should be developed together. Sacred Groves, Indian communities of Tai origin, Anugunj (showing the stories of different communities) are some examples of possible joint collaboration.

To conclude, some issues relevant to the Thai Cultural Centre have been discussed keeping in view globalization and other theoretical aspects in various fields of culture. In some cases, activities of some cultural organizations like IGRMS (National Museum of Mankind), Bhopal, have been cited as examples which have good potentiality in Thailand. While the antiquity of Indo-Thai cultural relations would historicize such relations, emphasis on documentation of Intangible Cultural Heritage both in India and Thailand including their heritage monuments and sites as well as the Indian Communities of Tai origin would help preserve the steady erosion of such aspects from collective memory. This will also provide a database of ICH of Third World Countries to assert the cause of Intellectual Property Rights in favour of the indigenous populations. Besides, the challenges in the tourism sector as well as in museology and archaeology were outlined. The solution to such challenges could be done by interactive workshop among Indian and Thai scholars together. Let us earnestly hope that the Thai Cultural Centre will not only act as a facilitating resource centre for Thai studies in India and Indian studies in Thailand, but also network the Indian diaspora in Thailand and the Thai diaspora in India, thus ensuring a cementing of the age-old bond between our countries.

REFERENCES

Boniface, Priscilla and Peter J. Fowler, *Heritage and Tourism in the Global Village*, London: Routledge, 1993.

Kelleher, Michael, Images of the Past: Historical Authenticity and Inauthenticity from Disney to Times Square, *CRM* 1(2): 6–19, 2004.

Tambiah, S.J., *World Conqueror and World Renouncer: A Study in Buddhism and Polity in Thailand Against a Historical Background*, New York: Cambridge University Press, 1976.

Consciousness and Psychic Factors in Pāli Buddhist Literature

RANA PURUSHOTTAM KUMAR SINGH

The quest for unravelling the contours of the human mind and consciousness has been endemic to the spirit of enquiry and investigation. It has resulted in the emergence of numerous theoretical formulations from different perspectives straddling various disciplines of knowledge, which attempt to address the multiple facets of consciousness. While neuroscientists dwell upon the biological bases of consciousness and ascribe it to the brain, there exists a concurrence among them on consciousness being a great mystery despite considerable advances in the knowledge of perception mechanisms. It is in this context that the rich repository of Buddhist philosophy appears as guiding light for the delineation of the trajectories of mind and consciousness.

According to Buddhist psychology the mind is a dynamic continuum which extends to an innumerable number of births. This has been hailed as the core of our existence. In fact, all psychological experiences such as pain and pleasure, sorrow and happiness, good and evil, life and death, are the consequences of our own thoughts and their resultant actions and are not attributable to external agencies.[1]

Mind is non-material. According to the *Abhidharma Kosha*, it is a part of the thinking process and a non-material entity.[2] The early Buddhist texts refer to mind as the originating point with regard to the mind of a layman and also culminating point as the liberated and purified mind of an enlightened man. The mind proceeds, thinks, dominates and creates worldly phenomena. Whatsoever there is of evil connected with evil, belonging to evil, all issues from mind. Whatever there is of good, connected with good, belonging to good, all issues from the mind.[3]

The Buddhist concept of the human mind or *citta* derives from root *citta* or *mana* which refers in the broadest way possible to mental processes, perceptive, intellectual, emotional, or imaginative.[4] In another sense, the term *citta* has been used in the sense of vision.[5] In several places, it denotes some sort of development or excellence of the faculty of thought or perception, as in the term *vipassa citta* in Pāli and *vipasha citta* in Vedic Sanskrit, which means wise or insightful or *sucetas* referring to the thoughtful.[6] Mind (*citta*), in Buddhist philosophy, has been defined as *ālambane cimteti iti cittaim*, the entity which thinks over the object. The thinking process becomes, in this way, the intimate part of personality. Establishing a link between rebirths, it assumes the function not of a string but a stream *nadi sota viya*. A similar explanation mind (*citta*) has been put forward by William James, who states that

> consciousness then does not appear to itself chopped up in bits. A word like chain, does not describe it well, as it presents itself in the first instant. It is nothing joined, it flows; a river or a stream are the metaphors by which it is naturally described. In talking of it, therefore, let us call it the stream of thought of consciousness or of subjective life.[7]

In Buddhism, our personality is the sum total of *nāma* (psychic properties) and *rūpa* (physical properties). *Nāma* is a combination of two non-material things like *citta* (mind) and *cetasika* (psychic factors). The term *nāma* + *rūpa* has been presented in a more simplified way. The term *nāma* represents the four non-material aggregates. These are *vedanā* (feeling), *saññā* (perception), *saṁkhāra* (volition) and *viññāṇa* (consciousness), whereas *rūpa* (physical aggregate) represents the body. It is due to the rise of inappropriate conditions that consciousness is known by various names: if consciousness arises because of eye and material shapes (*rūpa*), it is known as visual consciousness.[8] Consciousness functions when the eye that is internal is intact and external forms (*rūpa*) come within its range, but without appropriate contact (*samaññāhāra*)—then there is no appearance of the appropriate type of consciousness. On the other hand, when the eye that is internal includes external form within its range, accompanied by the appropriate contact, then there is an appearance of the appropriate type of consciousness.[9]

The function of consciousness begins from the stage of *phassa* (contact). Understanding of *phassa* is of more immediate importance with reference to the conditioning of feeling (*vedanā*) by *phassa* (contact) and the consequent conditioning of perception (*saññā*) by *vedanā* in the normal course of human consciousness.[10] *Vedanā* (feeling) is specifically said to have both a physical (*kāyika*) and mental (*cetasika*) aspect, and is considered to be of three types; pleasant (*sukha*), painful (*dukkha*) and equanimity (*upekkhā*). In another way, there are six type of *vedanā* (feelings) based on consciousness, such as feelings based on consciousness of eye, ear, and nose, tongue, body and mind respectively.[11]

Pleasant feelings too are related to the sense-organs. Pleasant feelings excite our attachment to objects, and rouse greed. Painful feelings excite latent anger and hatred. The saints who want to master passions have to eliminate three features connected with these feelings—the tendency to attachment in pleasant feeling, the tendency to revulsion in painful feelings, and the tendency to ignorance in natural feeling.

Apart from *vedanā* (feelings) as an important mental faculty, there are three other mental faculties which are dependent on each other and form an essential part of personality. These are the *saṁkhāra* (volition) *viññāṇa* (consciousness) and *saññā* (perception). These four concepts are seen as the key to the understanding of a comprehensive group of mental phenomena in Buddhism. In fact, some scholars have even compared the Buddhist analysis to the tripartite divison of the mind into cognition, conation, and affection. This tripartite divison is of crucial importance in understanding the Buddhist concept of mind, which considers *vedanā* (feelings) as the affective dimension of experience disposition, volition (*saṁkhāra*) as the conative dimensions and *saññā* (perception) and consciousness (*viññāṇa*) as the cognitive aspects, respectively.

In a deeper sense, all four mental aggregates are present in all the states of mind. Thus a mental factor like volition is not a separate entity, but is inseparably associated with the other factors. In this manner, the three dimensions of experience are the product of abstract analysis, with all three aspects being found in all states of consciousness and behaviour.

I now becomes worthwhile to throw light on the third mental entity that is *saññā* (perception). The term *saññā* is interpreted alternatively as conceptual activity. *Saññā* or perception establishes the cognitive apprehension of full-fledged material objects, The total perception of any external object is the result of an organic integration of the raw sensation. The character synthesis of 'raw' sense data is what this cognitive function realizes. Hence, *saññā* (perception) is a dharma which results from the synthesis of the raw sensations (*vedanā*) as there are integrated into an organic and sense-making 'whole'. *Saññā* (perception) then seems to have in phenomenological terms, a noematic character, as the organic and sense making 'presence' in consciousness of a distinct object.[12] This function which generates *saññā* (preception) is to be ascribed to the dharma of *viññāṇa*, the last of the *khandhas* to be explained as the last of the five *khandhas* (aggregates). In the *Abhidharmakosha, saññā* (perception) is defined as *nimittodgrahaṇātmika* or as distinct apprehension and discernment of objective determination.[13]

In another sense, *saññā* (perception) as resulting from the function of the mind is defined as *visayanimittagrahaṇa.*[14] Here *saññā* is construed as the result of 'comprehending' and thus synthesizing (*saṁgrahaṇa*) the mark (*nimitta*) and differentiations (*visesha*) among the sense matters (*rūpa-visaya*) which have been 'presented' by the sense-organ. The term *saññā* is divided into two types, *paṭigha saññā* and *adhivacana saññā.*[15] *Saññā* that arises out of contact with the sense-organs is described as *paṭigha saññā. Adhivacana saññā* is of a nominal character and includes sense images and concepts. Perception can be of six hands: of visual form, of sound, of smell, of taste, of bodily sensation and of images.[16]

The next significant non-material entity of our personality is *saṁkhāra* which is designed as 'volitive forces' or 'volitive information'. The *skandha* comprises a vast spectrum of both mental and non-mental forces, some of them associated with the cognitive acts already defined as *vedanā* and *saññā*, and many of them representing either instinctive or subconscious proclivities which operate on the basis of various sources of 'kārmic' causation. The *Dhammasaṁgaṇi* reduces the aggregates of dhammas to three main groups, thus including *vedanā* and *saññā* within the division of the *saṁkhāras* which are taken in general as 'mental functions'. In general, the *saññā* and *vedanā* are considered as *skandhas* in their own right, whereas *saṁkhāras* are restricted to all such operations of the human being in a more or less direct way to the realms of volition. Thus, the most significant of the *saṁkhāra* (volition) is the intentional act of the will which, of course, is strictly associated with such cognitive acts as are performed by the senses and the mind. This act of 'willing intention' is termed *cetanā*. Hence *cetanā* is the *saṁkhāra par excellence*, and as such is the foundation of *karma* which is morally imputable and 'remunerable' through the 'kārmic' cycle of causation. *Cetanā*, however, though the most significant of the *saṁkhāra*, is after all the first in a long list of forty-eight functions, with some of them directly associated with acts of consciousness (*citta saṁpayauttasaṁkhāra*) and then characterized as carriers of 'mental intentionality'. They can be rendered also as 'mental forces' indicating here their ever underlying association with the will. Of these, *cetasikas*—or *cittasaṁprayukta-saṁkāras* (or volitive function associated with acts of conscious-ness)—some are nothing but mere functions of *manas* (*viññāṇa* or mind faculty) inasmuch as they are 'commanded' by the will (*cetanā*); whereas others are innate propensities which 'predispose' or incline the will towards the position of certain actions. The first are cognitive functions ordered and directed by the will; the second, on the contrary, are inner proclivities which push and gravitate on the will.

According to the *Visuddhimagga*, the first are karma-forming forces (*abhisaṁkharaṇa-saṁkhāra*) in that they are posited and commanded by the will and thus become the object of moral retribution; they are actively kārmic and thus morally imputable as either evil (*akusala*) or good (*kusala*) deeds.[17] The second kind of 'force', those which 'predispose' and 'impel' the will are karma formed forces (*abhisaṁkhata-saṁkhāra*). In this way, the *saṁkhārakhandha* (volitional aggregate) is an active force and reactive in function, whereas *saṁkhāra* (volition) counted as the 'second link' in the 'interdependent chain of origination' designates all the passive potential (mental and physical) which, as released by death, provides the basis for rebirth.[18]

The fifth aggregate of personality is *viññāṇa*. In its nature, it is the subtlest and by the same token the most important of all the five *khaṁdhas* (aggregates). In brief, it can be said that *viññāṇa* (consciousness) is the basic concept of Buddhist psychology and consequently plays the most important role in Buddhist soteriology, since it is based on its 'purification' (*visuddhi*).[19] *Vijñāṇa* (consciousness) is the essential ground without which no *vedanā* (feeling) and *saññā* (perception) can emanate. No mental force, as described in the *saṁkhāra khanda* (volitional aggregate), can function without *viññāṇa* (consciousness).[20] *Vedanā* (feelings), *saññā* (perception), and *cetanā* (volitive acts) are not considered *dravya* (element) but functional factors (*krityika dharma*), and come to manifestation only through the interaction and 'contact' (*phassa*) between the *rūpa* (subtle and gross, sense-organs and the fifth aggregate *viññāṇa*).[21]

After the study of the five aggregates, it becomes imperative to discuss the function of mind. Our mind functions through its faculties. For example, the perception of objects in the external world is influenced by our desire and interest. If our 'perception' of object is influenced by our desires, it would be necessary to train our senses to see these objects as they are, rather than project on to them what is really not there. The Buddha does not say, like the idealists, that the external world is a mere creation of the imagination. Rather, while accepting the reality of the sensory process, it is pointed out that to a greater degree our perceptions are mixed with non-sensory conceptual and imaginative component. The Buddha is making two significant points here: first he is saying that we should not get excited by sensory stimuli and our passions and attachments should be restrained; he is also saying that even our perception of objects and our responses to sensory stimuli are shot through with our psychological make-up. The Middle Length Sayings present the emergence of perception in this manner; when the eye that is internal is intact and external visible forms come within its range, followed by an appropriate act of attention on the part of the mind, there emerges perceptual consciousness.[22] Thus, visual cognition is a causal process depending on three factors: an unimpaired sense-organ, external visible forms and an act of attention. Here, the term used for coginition is *viññāṇa*.[23] The process is not only true of the eye (*cakkhu*) but also five other cases of the ear (*sota*), nose (*ghana*), tongue (*jihvā*), body (*kāya*) and mind (*mano*) respectively. It is when all these conditions are satisfied that one sees the emergence of the cognitive process. In this context, the word *viññāṇa* has a cognitive import and is really a reference to the emergence of cognitive consciousness.

It is pertinent to note without describing the function of consciousness, one cannot understand the theory of mind in Buddhist philosophy. As has been mentioned earlier that the mind is a changing process, the process manifests itself in two levels or streams—the *vīthi citta* or conscious mind and *bhavaṁga citta* or the subconscious mind. The *bhavaṁga citta* (subconscious mind) is subconsciously active. It is referred to as a state of subliminal activity,[24] an activity that takes place below the threshold of the conscious mind, an activity of which, therefore, there is no awareness to the conscious mind. The conscious (*vīthi citta*) holds only one thought or idea at a time, whereas the subconscious or unconscious (*bhavaṁga citta*) holds all impressions of all thoughts, idea and experiences that enter and leave the conscious *vīthi citta*. The *bhavaṁga citta* thus functions as a valuable mental impression. Now the question arises as to how the *vīthi citta* (conscious mind) and *bhavaṁga citta* (unconscious mind) function. As we know, the mind is an endless succession of thoughts, each following the next with such rapidity of succession as to give it the semblance of something permanent and stable, whereas in reality it is not a unit but a process, with the difference that it is limited process—a process of seventeen thought moments each following the other.

The first moment, called (*bhavaṁga atita*) is the past unconscious. The stage is prior to the running of the conscious process, the stage when the conscious *vīthi citta* is in abeyance and the stream of the unconscious *bhavaṁga citta* is flowing undisturbed.

The second process is called *bhavaṁga-calana* (vibration of the *bhavaṁga*).This stage comes after a conscious thought has subsided and before the next arises. The mind is then in the *bhavaṁga* (unconscious) state for a very short while. The *bhavaṁga* flow now begins to vibrate.[25] This vibration lasts for one thought moment before it subsides. This is the result of the stimulus or object trying to force its attention on the conscious mind by impending the flow of the *bhavaṁga* stream of consciousness.

The third stage is called *bhavaṁga upaccheda* (arrest of the *bhavaṁga*), the stage when the stream of the *bhavaṁga citta* is arrested or cut-off.[26] As result, the *vīthi citta* or conscious process arises and begins to flow, but this stimulus or object is not yet cognized by it.

The fourth stage is called *pañcadvārāvajjana* (five door apprehending). This is the stage when a beginning is made by the conscious *vīthi citta* to cognize the object which has arrested the flow of the unconscious *bhavaṁga*. This stage is called *pañca-dvārāvajjana* because there is a turning round to find out through which of the five sense-doors the stimulus is emerging. There is thus attention towards the stimulus or object through one of the five senses—channels of sight, hearing, smell, taste and touch.[27]

The fifth stage is called *pañcaviññāṇa* (five-fold consciousness). Now follows a consciousness of the kind that apprehends the particular sense impression caused by the stimulus. If it is a sight, it is *cakkhu viññāṇa* or visual consciousness that works. If it is a sound, it is *sota viññāṇa* or auditory consciousness that work. In this way, with respect to each other of the sense-organs, there is particular sense consciousness which begins to work.

The sixth stage is called *sampaṭicchana* (reception). It is the thought moment which occurs when the sense impression caused by the stimulus is properly received.[28]

The seventh stage is *santiraṇa* (investigation). After the function of receiving there arises the function of investigation. This thought process performs the function of investigating with discrimination the stimulus or object which causes the sense-impression.[29]

The eighth stage is called *voṭṭhapana* (decision), when a decision is made regarding the stimulus which caused the sense impression.[30]

The stages from ninth to fifteenth are collectively called *javana* (thought-impulsions). This stage lasts for seven thought moments. It is the stage of introspection followed by action. These mental states, unlike the previous mental states, run for several thought moments and their one function is to impel.[31] These are impulsions which flash forth at the climax of a process of consciousness of the *vīthi citta*. Hence one is now fully conscious of the object or stimulus in all its relations, this being the stage of maximum cognition. It is at this stage that the *kamma* begins to operate for good or bad, for this is the stage when the element of free will is present. *Javana* is the only stage where man is relatively free to think and to decide.

The sixteenth and seventeenth stages are referred to as *tadālambana* (registration of experiences). These are the two resultant thought moments following immediately after the *javana* thought moments. Their only function is to register the impression made by *javana* thought moment.[32] They are not an integral part of the conscious *vīthi* process but are merely a recall of an experience that is passing away.

According to Buddhist psychology, *citta* (consciousness) is ever dynamic, its forms or states are in perpetual flux like the waves of ocean. In this sense, it is momentary but its essence is eternal. This *citta* consciousness is the principal basis of phenomenal reality. In other words, the cause of all kinds of evolution is *citta* consciousness. Once the function of *citta* consciousness has started, it is said that it bears a relationship with all the three times; past, present and future. Through the forces gathered by its past activities, it continues its present activities, which produce similar forces to propel it to the future ones. Thus the phenomenal process keeps going until there is a deliberate and systematic attempt by man to degenerate craving (*taṇhā*) and achieve a state of *nirvāna*. This explains the causal link between any two states of *citta* (consciousness). And it also explains the origin of consciousness with three moral roots and three immoral roots.

Further, an individual's reasons, belief, desire, and purpose are motivations of moral or immoral actions. All these elements are individual-based and thus intrinsic to man. These factors determine the type and course of action one wants to perform. Moreover, man has a certain degree of control over these factors, for he is free to train or culture his mind and interpret a particular situation in such a way that his existing belief or desire changes radically. In this sense, he has control over these elements and freedom in exercising choice about action. An important point in exercising our freedom is the correct understanding of the nature of action, its ethical consequences, and social implications. Thus, right cognition of things is a necessary condition for the realization of values. The Buddhist theory, which explains that karmas mature in the present and the present ones in the future, thus explains the suffering or happy life of a person in the present for which, to the best of one's knowledge, one has performed any karma. The fact of inequality among human beings is also explained on this line. The Buddhist kārmic discipline aims at inculcating highest universal moral values on secular lines.

In the *Dighanikaya*, Buddha talks about the ethical consequences of action. Man's present condition, such as being inferior or superior, beautiful or ugly, and of good or bad nature, is attributed to one's past action.[33]

In the *Aṁguttara Nikaya*, Buddha talks about the causal correlation between actions—mental, bodily, and linguistic—the results of the maturation of which is called the law of karma.[34] Here in the *Majjhimanikaya*, Buddha explains the inequality among human beings in all respects. Their differing psychological, biological, economic and social conditions, i.e. karma keeps a man in good or bad state.[35]

NOTES

1. Kammassaka Satta, Kammadāyadā, Kammayoni, Kammabandhu, Kamma paṭisarṇā—*M.N.*, I, pp. 25.
2. *Citta caitta dharmāh, arūpino dharmāh—Ab. K,* II. 34.
3. a. *Manopubbaṅgamā dhammā, DP*, 11.
   b. *Manah eva manushyānaṁ kāraṇam bandhamokshayoh —Brahmabindupanishat*, 144.
4. *Aṁguttaranikāya* — II, p. 177.
5. *Origin of Indian Psychology*, p. 101.
6. *Rg*., 1.64.36.
7. William James, *The Principles of Psychology*. Here I owe it to Claudio Naranjo and Robert E. Ornstein, *On the Psychology of Meditation*, Penguin Books, p.189.
8. a. *Cakkhuñca paticca rūpe ca uppajjati cakkhuviññāṇaṁ—Saṁyutta-nikāya*, II, p. 73.
   b. *Cakkuñcāvuso, paticca rūpe ca uppajjati cakkhuviññāṇaṁ—M.N.*, I, p. 158.
   c. *Cakkhuṁ ceva rūpaṁ ca, sotaṁ ceva saddaṁ ca, . . . kāyo ceva photabbā ca mano ceva dhammā ca. — D.N.*, III, p. 670.
9. *Cakkuṁvacuso, paticca rūpe ca uppajjati cakkhuviññāṇaṁ—M.N.*, I, 158.
10. a. *Cakkhuṁ ca paticca rūpe ca uppajjati cittaṁ mano manomānasaṁ hadayaṁ paṇdaraṁ mano manāyatanaṁ manidriyaṁ viññāṇaṁ viññānakkhandho tajjā cakkhuviññāṇadhātu—Vibhango*, p. 109.
    b. *Lokassa, bhikkave, samudayañca aṭṭhangamañca desessāmi Samyuttanikayo*, p. 93, V.R.I.
    c. *Kittāvattā pana bhante paticcasamuppādakusalo bhikkhu ti alam vacanāyā ti—M.N.*, III, 110.
    d. *Ehayime, āvuso vedanā kāyā—cakkhusamphassajā, vedanā, sota samphassajā vedanā ghāṇasamphassajā vedanā jihvāsamphassajā vedanā—M.N.*, I., 65.
11. *Assadaṁ assādatovedanā aniccātipassati*, see, W.F. Jayasuriya, *The Psychology and Philosophy of Buddhism*, 1963, p. 16, de silva, op. cit., p. 17.
12. *Sañjānāti sañjānāti to kho āvuso tasmā saññati vuccati nilakampi sañjānāti, pitakaṁpi sañjānāti, lohitakaṁpi sañjānāti—M.N.*, p. 372.

13. '*Saṁjñā nimittodgrahaṇātmika*'
Yāvannilapitādirgharastripureh, mitra amitra sukhadukkha ādinimittohaṇmasou saṅjañā,
—*Adhidhamakosha*—.14.
14. *Saṅjañā saṁjañanaṁ vishayanimittodgraha*—*A.K.*, II, p. 187.
15. *Esā paṭighasanphassajā saññā ti vuttā*—*Samohavinodani*, pp. 20.
16. *Cakkhusamphassajā saññā, sotasamphassajā saññā, ghāṇasamphassjā saññā, jihvāsaṁphassaja saññā, Kāyasaṁphassajā saññā, manosamphassjā saññā. Evaṁ chabbidhena saññākkhandho*—Vibhango, pp. 32.
17. '*yaṁ kiñci abhisaṁkhāraṇalakkhaṇaṁ sabbaṁtaṁ ekato katvā saṁikhārakkhaṁdho veditabbo' ti*—*Visuddhimaggo*, p. 388.
18. Ibid.
19. *Sabbapāpassa akaraṇaṁ, kusalassa upasaṃpadā Sacittapariyodapanaṁ, etaṁ Buddhānasāsanaā*—*D.N.*, II, 305.
20. *Dharmayātanadhātvākhyāh sahavijñāyaptyasaṁskritaih*—*A.K.*, I, 15, pp. 50.
21. *Vedanā cetanā saṁjañā chandah sparsho matih smritih Manaskārodhimoksha samadhih sarvacetasi*—*A.K.*, II. 24, p. 186.
22. *Cakkhuṅca pajānāti, rūpe ca pajānāti, yañca tadubhayaṁ paticca uppajjati saṁyojanaṁ*—*M.N.*, I, p. 80.
23. *Ghānaṁ aparibhinnaṁ hoti, jihvā aparibhinnā, hoti bāhirā ca dhammā na āpāthaṁ agacchanti no ca tajjo samanāhāro hoti neva tāva tajjassa viññāṇbhāgassa pātubhāvo hoti*—*M.N.*, I, p. 251.
24. *Avicchedappavattihetubhāvena bhavassa aṅgabhāvo bhavaṁgakiccaṁ*—*Vibhāvani*, p. 95
25. *Ghaṭṭite aññavathumhi aññanissitakampanaṁ Ekābaddhena hotīti sakkharopamayā vade*—*Adhidhammatthasangaho*, p. 306.
Tadā cakkhussāpāthagati rūpe rūpaṁ paṭicca cakkhupasādassa ghaṭṭanā hoti—*Visuddhimaggo*, p. 320.
Tattha paṭhamattaṁ bhavaṁgasaṁtatiṁ catentaṁ viya uppajjatiti bhavaṁgacalanaṁ—*Vibhāvinitikā*.
26. *Dutiyaṁ tassa acchijjanākāsena uppajjanato bhavaṁgupacchedo ti voharanti.*—*Vibhāvanitikā*.
27. *Āvajjanaṁ cittasantānassa āvatthanaṁ, taṁ vā āvajjeti, āvaṭṭheti, āvaṭṭhati vā taṁ ettha etenā ti vā, āvajjanaṁ bhavaṅgavīthito okkamitvā ārammaṇantarā mmaṇatarā bhimukhaṁ pavattatīti attho, āvajjeti vā ārammaṇanatari, ābhogaṁ korotiti āvajjanam*—*Paramatthadīpani*, pp. 105.
28. *Sampaṭicchiyate sampaṭicchanaṁ. "Cakkhuviññāṇadhātuyā uppajjitvā niruddhasamanatarā uppajjati cittaṁ manomanāsaṁ sampaṭicchanavasena pavattati veditabbā*—*Visuddhimaggo*—320.
29. *Sammā tīranaṁ, santīraṇaṁ, tulanaṁ, vimaṁsansṁ, ti attho.*
—*Abhidhammatthasamgaho*, 226.
30. *Visuṁ visuṁ avicchinditvā ṭhapanaṁ voṭṭhappanaṁ*—*Abhidammatthaṁgaho*—226.

31. *Javanaṁ pana rajjana-virajjanādivasena itthāniṭṭhavibhāgaṁ karotiti ālambanarasaṁ javaneva anubhavatiti vuttaṁ—Parmatthadipani*, p. 105.
32. *Taṁāranmaṇaṁ etassā ti tadārammaṇaṁ, yam javanena gahitārammaṇaṁ tasseva gahitā tadārammaṇaṁ nāma ti hi vuttam—Parmatthadipani.*
33. *So dibbena cakkhunā visuddhena atikkantamanussakena satte passati cavamāne, upajjamāne, hine paṇite suvaṇṇe duvaṇṇe sugate duggate yathā kammupage satte payana ti—D.N.*, p. 73.
34. *Kammassakomhi kammdāyado kammayoni, kammabaṁdhu, kammapaṭisasaṇā, yaṁ kammaṁ karissāmi kalyāṇaṁ vā pāpakaṁ vā tassa dāyado bhavissāmi ti abhinnaṁ paccevekhitabbaṁ itthiyā vā purisevā a, gahaṭṭhena vā pabbajjitena vā—A.N.*, p. 335.
35. *Kammassaka mānava sattā, kammadāyadā kammayoni, kammabandhu, kammapaṭisaraṇā, kammaṁ satte vibhajati yadidam hinappanitāya— M.N.*, III, p. 250.

SELECT BIBLIOGRAPHY

Abhidhammatthasaṁgaho, ed. Rev Revatadhamma, Varanasi: Varanasi Sanskrit University, 1967.

Abhidhammatthavibhavaniṭikā, ed. Rev Revatadhamma, Varanasi: Buddha Swadhyaya Satra, 1965.

Abhidhannāvatāro, ed. Prof. M. Tiwari, Delhi, 1987.

Abidharmakosham, ed. Swami Dwarkadas Shastri, Varanasi: Buddha Bharti, 1987.

Aṁguttara Nikāya, ed. Bhikkhu J. Kassapa, Nalanda Edition, 1960.

Cullavagga, ed. Bikkhu J. Kassapa, Nalanda Edition, 1956.

David, Mrs. C.A.F. Rhys, *The Birth of Indian Psychology and its Development in Buddhism*, Delhi: Munshiram Manoharlal 1978.

Dhammasaṁgani, ed. B.J. Kassapa, Nalanda Edition, 1960.

Dhātukathā, ed. B.J. Kassapa, Nalanda Edition, 1960.

Dighanikāya, ed. Swami Dwarkadas Shastri, Varanasi: Bauddha Bharti, 1966.

Dhammapada, ed. Prof. Sanghasen Singh, Delhi: University Press, 1977.

Early Buddhist Philosophy, Alfonso Verdo, Delhi: Motilal Banarsidass, 1985.

Guenther, H.V., *Philosophy and Psychology in the Abhidhamma*, New Delhi: Motilal Banarsidass, 1957.

Jayatileke, K.N., *Facets of Buddhist Thought*, Kandy, Sri Lanka: Buddhist Publication Society, 1971.

Kalupahana, D.J., *Buddhist Philosophy, A Historical Analysis*, Honolulu: University Press of Hawaii, 1976.

Kathāvatthu, ed. B.J. Kassapa, Nalanda, Edition, 1961.

Majjhima Nikāya, ed. Vipassana Research Institute, Igatpuri, Nasik, 1995.

Millindapañho, ed. Dwarkadas Shastri, Varanasi: Bauddha Bharti, 1979.

Mahāvagga, ed. Bikkhu J. Kassapa, Nalanda Edition, 1956.

Paṭṭhāna, ed. B.J. Kassapa, Nalanda Edition, 1961.
Pātanjal Yogastura, ed Dr. Pavan Kumari Gupta, Delhi: Eastern Book Linkers, 1979.
Puggalapaññatti, ed. J. Kassapa, Nalanda Edition 1960.
Reat, N. Ross, *The Origins of Indian Psychology*, Berkeley: Asian Humanities Press, 1951.
Saṁyuttanikāya, Jagatpuri Nasik: Vipassana Research Institute, 1994.
Sammohavinodani, ed. Prof. S. Mukherjee, Nalanda Edition, 1961.
Stcherbatsky, Th, *The Central Conception of Buddhism*, Delhi: Motilal Banarsidass, 1974.
Suttanipata, ed. Rev. Dhammarakkhita, Delhi: Motilal Banarsidass, 1977.
Thera Gatha, ed. Bhikku. J. Kassapa, Nalanda Edition, 1958.
Upanishatsangraha, ed. Pt. Jagadashashastri, Delhi: Motilal Banarsidass, 1970.
Vibhanga, ed. B.J. Kassapa, Nalanda Edition, 1960.
Visuddhi Maggo, ed. Pt. Badarinath Shukla, Varanasi: Varanasi Sanskrit University, 1969.
Vijnaptimatratasiddhi, ed. Pt. Ramashankara Tripathi, Varanasi: Varanasi Sanskrit University, 1972.
Yamaka, ed. B.J. Kassapa, Nalanda Edition, 1961.
Yogavartika, Vijanabhikshu, ed. T.S. Rukmani, New Delhi: Munshiram Manoharlal, 1983.
Yagavasishthah, ed. V.L. Sharma Panzikar, Delhi: Motilal Banarsidass, 1984.

Dvaravati: Early Buddhist Kingdom in Central Thailand

PHASOOK INDRAWOOTH

Literary and archaeological evidence confirms that between the seventh and eleventh centuries central Thailand was the homeland of a Buddhist kingdom called 'Dvaravati'. In the seventh century, Chinese historians and pilgrims to India spoke of a kingdom they called To-lo-po-ti situated to the west of Isanapura (Cambodia) and to the east of Sri Ksetra (Burma).[1] The Chinese name for this polity was interpreted as representing the Sankrit word *Dvaravati* meaning 'which has gates', and in 1964 this interpretation was confirmed by two inscribed silver coins found at Nakhon Pathom.[2]

Dvaravati kingdom developed out of earlier, probably Austro-Asiatic-speaking,[3] chiefdoms of prehistoric central Thailand. Based on archaeological evidence, many Iron Age sites in Thailand, such as Rim Khwae Noi, Ban Don Ta Phet, and Khok Plub in the Maklong-Tha Chin valleys, reveal evidence of exchange with India during the Maurya-Sunga period (*c*. 350–50 BC).

During the protohistoric period, contemporaneous with the Indo-Roman period in India (*c*. 50 BC-AD 300), trade relations between India and the local people in central Thailand had been extensive. India had an active trade with Roman Empire. By this time, local rulers in Thailand accepted the surperiority of Indian cultural paradigms and saw the value of Indian concepts as a means of legitimizing their own political ends. They therefore brought to their courts the priests and literati who introduced many elements of Indian culture to the Dvaravat people, such as the system of coinage, sealings, Pali and Sanskrit languages, religious beliefs, town planning, art and architecture, ceramics, concepts of state and kingship, and a variety of musical instruments and dances.

DVARAVATI, THE EARLY BUDDHIST KINGDOM IN CENTRAL THAILAND (MAPS 1-3)

The seventh century saw a large number of moated sites located along the margins of the Central Plain. According to Vanasin and Supajanya, the sea level was higher at that time, and so these

Map 1: Main sites in South-East Asia during the Dvaravati period.

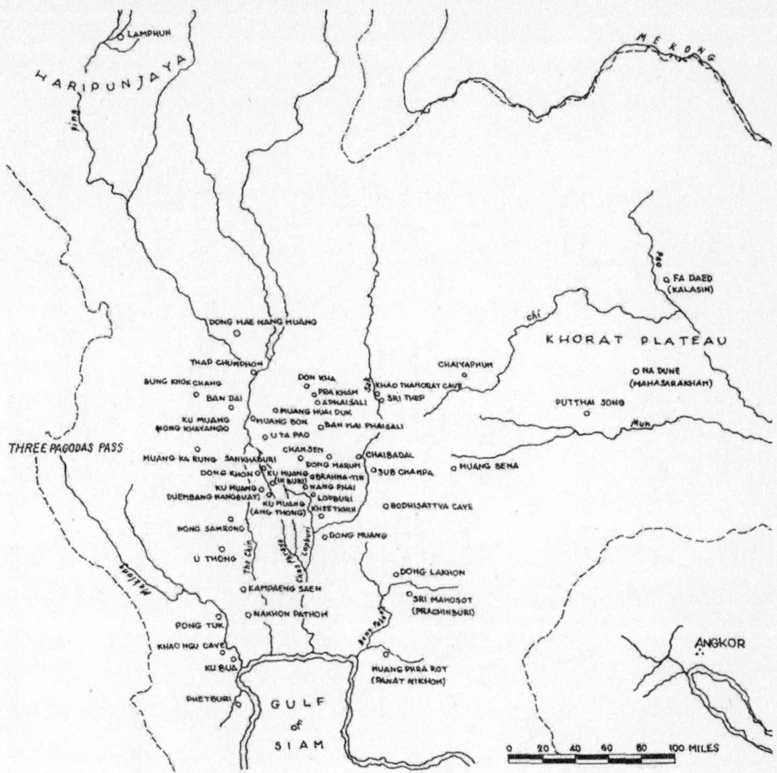

Map 2: The Main Dvaravati sites in Central Thailand.

settlements were accessible by boat. Most sites were also located near rivers which supplied water to the moats.[4] Large religious buildings were constructed within the moats, while small ones lay outside the enclosures. Major moat-encircled sites have been found in the Meklong-Ta Chain, Lopburi-Pasak, and Bang Pakong valleys. Some sites such as Dong Khon, Muang Bon, U Ta Pao, and Thap Chumphon, were located near the Chao Phraya river. Sites in the Meklong-Ta Chin valleys include a number of important Dvaravati towns such as U-Thong, Nakhon Pathom, and Ku Bua. This paper will concentrate on Nakhon Pathom.

Nakhon Pathom, situated near the west bank of the Ta Chin river, is nearer the Gulf coast than U-Thong. This was a great town covering an area of 3,700 by 2,000 m (Fig. 1). Situated almost in the centre of

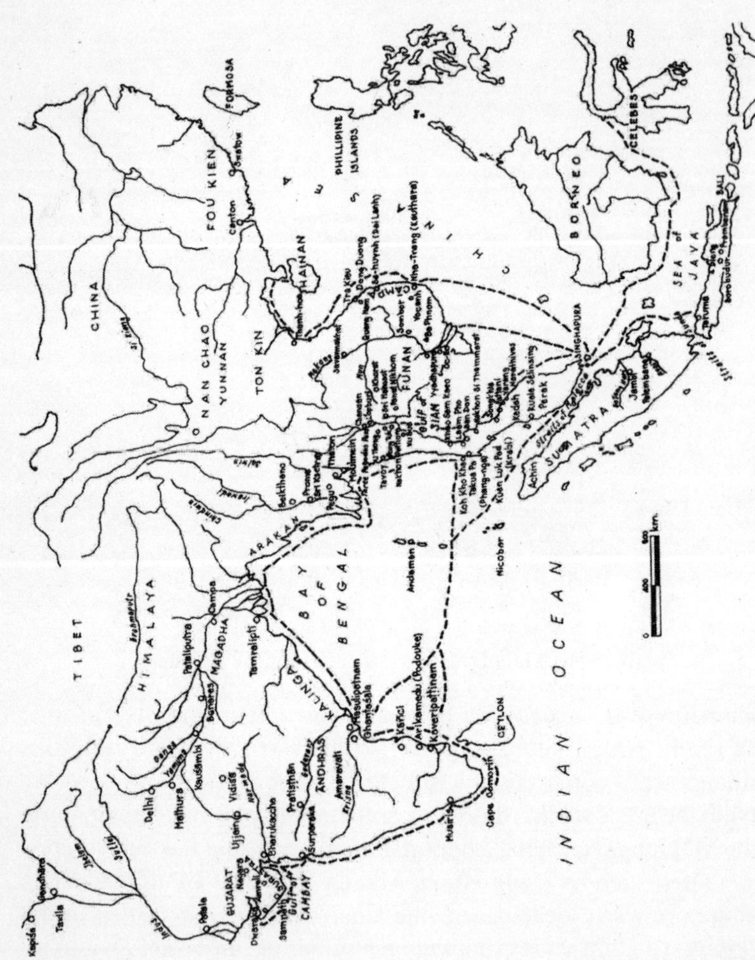

Map 3: Sea routes and ancient ports in India and South-East Asia.

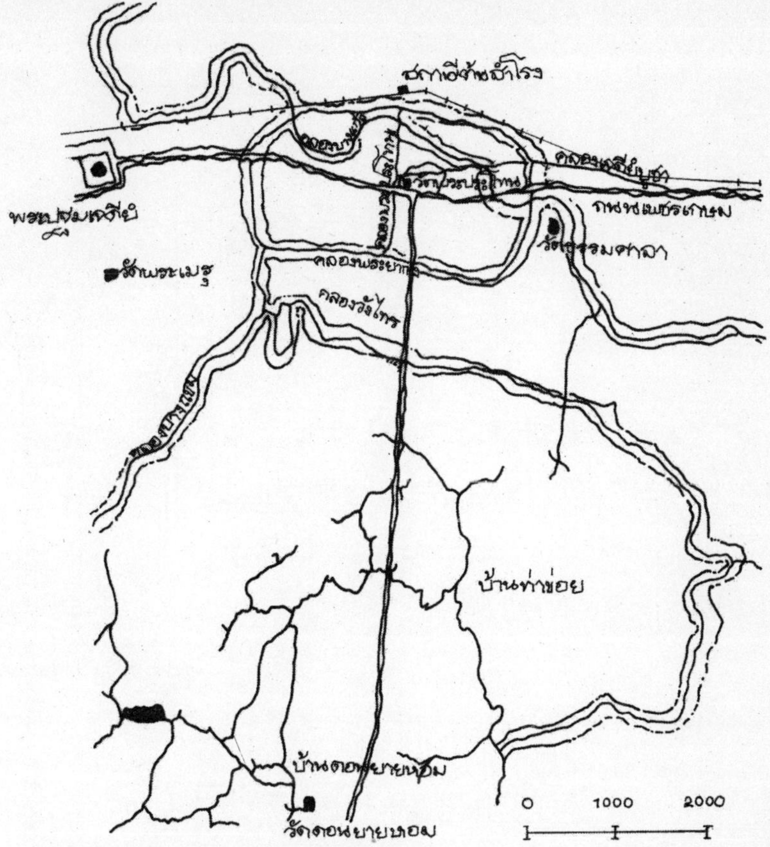

Fig. 1: Town plan of Nakhon Pathom, the capital Dvaravati Kingdom.

the town, the central mound was all that remained of the ancient brick monument of Chula Paton. Excavations here by the late Pierre Dupont have provided the most important contribution to our knowledge of Dvaravati architecture.[5] Here we see one of the most characteristic types of Dvaravati monument (Figs. 2, 3). This brick structure was modified several times. In its first state, it consisted of a central square platform with little indentations. It was ornamented on each face by five standing Buddhas of stucco, placed in niches. It stood on its own base, of the same plan but a little wider, with facings ornamented with mouldings and, on the projecting angles, *makaras* in relief. The whole was supported on a rectangular terrace.

Fig. 2: Plan of ancient brick monument of Chula Paton Chedi, Nakhon Pathom Province (the first and second stages).

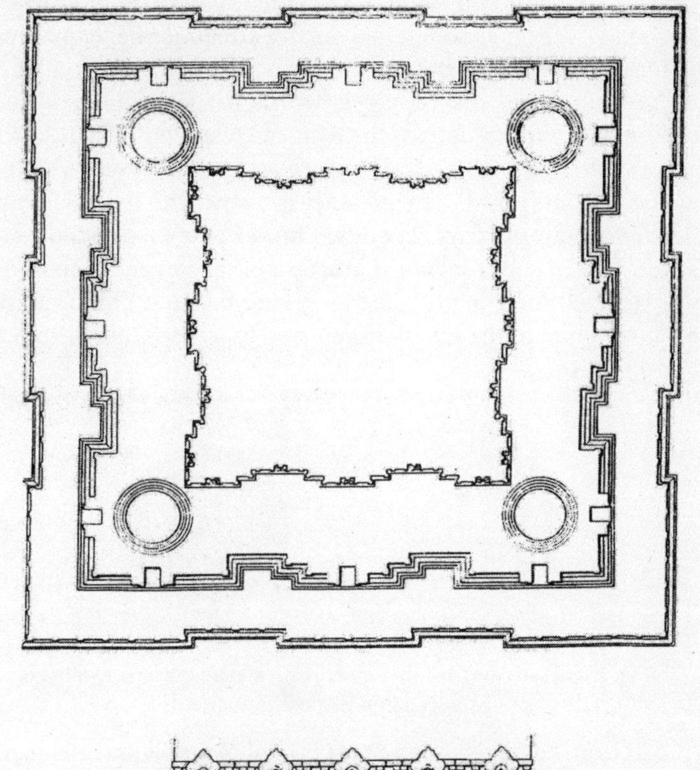

Fig. 3: Plan of Chula Pathon Chedi (the third stage).

This was ornamented with panels bearing alternatively a *Garuda* and an elephant. Four axial flights of steps, with the bottom step semi-circular, gave access to the terrace. They were flanked by lions carved on the facing, and had balustrades issuing from the mouths of monsters. In the second stage, the decoration of the base was simplified. In the third stage, new Buddha images were substituted for the old ones in the niches, and changes were made simplifying the much enlarged terrace.

The most important small finds from Nakhon Pathom are two inscribed silver coins found in a small earthen jar beneath a ruined sanctuary at Nern Hin, west of Pra Praton.[6] On the reverse of each coin are engraved the Sanskrit words *sridvaravatisvarapunya* meaning 'meritorious deed of the King of Dvaravati'. On the obverse of one coin is a 'vase of plenty' (*purnaghata*) from which two creepers sprout (Fig. 4). On the other is a cow with its calf, symbols of fertility and prosperity. Coedes, who read the inscriptions, stated that they are in south Indian characters of the seventh century, and he recognized their importance as giving the first confirmation of the actual name of the kingdom referred to by the Chinese pilgrims as To-lo-po-ti.[7]

Fig. 4: Silver coins bearing inscription and auspicious symbols, from Nakhon Pathom Province.

Apart from being regarded as the capital of the Dvaravati kingdom, ancient Nakhon Pathom had an important role as a trading centre, and a large number of terracotta seals and sealings (Fig. 5) and some amulets for merchants are among the finds from this site.[8] Other important finds are over 30 pieces of stone *dharmacakras*. One has two figures of crouching deer to symbolize the First Sermon in the Deer Park at Sarnath[9] (Fig. 6). There are as well images of the Buddha made of stone and bronze. Thus the Buddhist monuments at Nakhon Pathom, including Pra Paton, emphasize its importance as a Buddhist centre during Dvaravati times. And the Pali texts engraved on some stone *dharmacakras* mostly saying *praticca-samuppada-sutta,* provide evidence that the Dvaravati people were familiar with the Pali canon.[10]

Later excavations in the occupation area have also expanded our knowledge of this site.[11] Many artefacts resemble earlier prehistoric objects, such as bronze ornaments, iron spears and spindle whorls.

Fig. 5: Terracotta seal bearing ship, symbol of sea-trade, from Nakhon Pathom Province.

Fig. 6: Stone Dharmacakra with figure of crouching deer, from Nakhon Pathom Province.

However, the settlement appears to have been founded around AD 800 and was probably abandoned when the river changed its course, not long after AD 1000.

MATERIAL CULTURE

The study of the archaeological remains in Central Thailand during the Dvaravati period provide a clear perspective of Dvaravati culture, which digested many elements of Indian culture, such as town plans, buildings, implements, domestic utensils, ornaments, and ceramics.

Although irregular moated sites have been noted in the dry north-east of Thailand during the late Iron Age,[12] the series of large moated towns (Fig. 1) along the margins of the Central Plains of Thailand during the Dvaravati period are undoubtedly due to a high degree of Indianization. On the Ganga plains of northern India, almost all the principal Iron Age sites were located on the river banks where the inhabitants erected clay embankments to prevent flood waters from entering the habitation area. During the Indian Iron Age (*c*. 700–350 BC) earth embankments and moats as flood protective devices are noted at sites such as Kausambi, Varanasi, and Pataliputra. During the Early Historic period (*c*. 350–50 BC) these were developed into substantial defensive ramparts. Pataliputra and Kausambi are examples where the clay embankments of the early phase, with certain modifications, were converted for defensive purposes.[13]

What we find in some Dvaravati towns is an improvement from the irregular, more or less circular or oval muclei found in earlier Iron Age sites, by extending the original circular site on to a wider area of land with new ramparts and moats such as at Muang Bon, Nakhon Sawan Province,[14] or by the grafting on of a secondary enclosure, as at Sri Thep[15] and at Muang Fa Daed, Kalasin Province.[16] At U-Thong, a stone wall for defence built on the top of a clay rampart could once be seen,[17] but is no longer standing.

During the Dvaravati period, houses were generally built of wood, while fired brick and laterite were used for religious structures. The larger Buddhist monuments, mostly of brick, were constructed within settlements, while smaller ones were outside the enclosures.

The distribution of a large number of uninscribed silver coins throughout the Dvaravati kingdom and in contemporary cities like the Pyu cities of Myanmar (Beikthano, Sriksetra and Halin), Mon (Pegu), and the ancient Funan port at Oc Eo, indicates that coinage was used in trade.[18] Most coins bear Indian symbols of kingship and prosperity, such as the rising sun, the *sankha* (conch shell), and *srivatsa*, the abode of Sri, goddess of fertility (Figs. 7, 8).

Fig. 7: Silver coin bearing rising sun and *srivatsa*, symbols of fertility and prosperity.

Fig. 8: Silver coin bearing sankha and srivatsa symbols of fertility and prosperity.

A large number of seals made of clay and other materials belonging to kings, royal officials, and private individuals as well as of administrative, mercantile and religious organizations, have been discovered in the main Dvaravati cities such as Nakhon Pathom (Fig. 5) and Chansen in Nakhon Sawan Province.[19] The writing on the seals is usually positive. Some seals have also been found with legends in intaglios, probably used for sealing documents.

Among the many artefacts unearthed by excavation in the occupation areas of the important Dvaravati towns such as Nakhon Pathom, a wide range of implements and domestic utensils are found.[20] These include polished stone axes, iron tools, and stone saddle querns and rollers (Fig. 9) derived from Indian prototypes.[21]

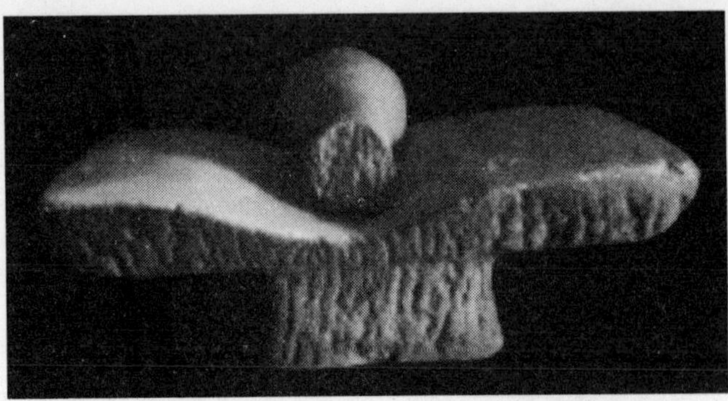

Fig. 9: Stone anvil and roller for grinding spices, from Muang Sri Thep, Petchaburi Province.

The latter were probably used for grinding spices such as garlic and pepper, and also foodstuffs.

Personal toilet items such as square or rectangular terracotta skin rubbers were found in excavations in the domestic areas of most Dvaravati cities, such as Sri Mahosot (Fig. 10), Prachinburi Province.[22] Such skin-rubbers were usually used in place of soap by Indians in the Ganga valley.

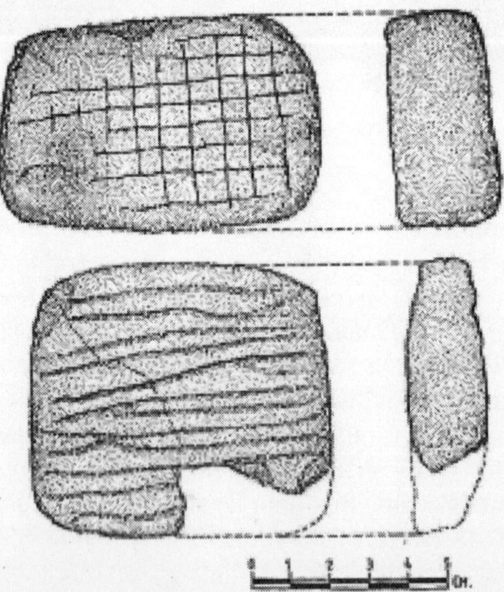

Fig. 10: Terracotta skin-rubber from Sri Mahosot, Pracinburi Province.

Fig. 11: Stucco image showing women, perhaps a princess with her attendant, from Ku Bua, Ratchaburi Province.

A wide range of personal ornaments have been reported, such as large flat tin and lead earrings, bronze bells, bronze rings and beads of glass, carnelian, agate and gold. The stucco images from Ku Bua, Ratchaburi Province, show women—perhaps a princess with her attendant—with elaborate hairstyles, large flat ear ornaments, and elegant clothing[23] (Fig. 11).

Many of the stucco human figures from Ku Bua display various court activities which include musicians (Fig. 12) and dancers (Fig 13). It is observed that the musical instruments as well as the dancing poses may have derived from the Indian prototypes.

Dvaravati ceramics are unglazed, mainly wheel-thrown, earthenwares fired in an open hearth rather than in a closed kiln. Analytical studies on Dvaravati pottery have revealed that the raw materials used by the potters were local and the pottery basically continued the forms of prehistoric period, such as the dish-on-stand; however, strongly carinated vessels with ridges become more noticeable and these perhaps follow Indian ceramic styles.

Jars with spouts (*kendi*), sprinklers (*kundika*), and small cups used as lamps (Figs. 14-16) also show close similarity both in shape and design to Indian prototypes of the early Common Era up to the

Fig. 12: Stucco images showing musicians, from Ku Bua, Ratchaburi Province.

Fig. 13: Stucco image showing dancer, from Ku Bua, Ratchaburi Province.

post-Gupta period, AD 700–800.[24] Western influences can also be seen in the terracotta Roman style lamps (Fig. 17) in household use during the Dvaravati period. They are thought to be local imitations

Figs. 14–17: Dvaravati ceramics: jar with spout - terracotta Roman lamp - carinated pot - small cups used as lamps

of bronze Roman lamps such as the one found at Pong Tuk (Fig. 18) in Kanchanaburi Province.[25]

Decorative techniques used by the Dvaravati potters include incised lines and waves, the use of cord and mat wrapped paddles, and impression with fingers or snail-shell edges.

Fig. 18: Bronze Roman lamp found at Pong Tuk, Kanchanaburi Province.

A technique of decorating pots in relief using carved stamps was also used by Dvaravati potters following a technique introduced by Indian potters of the Gupta and the post-Gupta periods.[26] Such stamped designs include human figures in different postures, animal figures, and flower motifs (Fig. 19). It is believed that the fashion for stamp-decorated pottery during the Gupta period was a local imitation of Roman stamped pottery such as Arretine ware,[27] some of which reached India along the maritime trade routes, as well as Hellenistic stamped pottery which had reached northern India from Afghanistan and Central Asia.

SOCIAL RELATIONS

Many of the stucco and terracotta architectural decorations from Ku Bua illuminate social relations during Dvaravati times.[28] The image

Fig. 19: Fragment of stamped pottery found at Nakhon Pathom Province.

of a princess with her attendant mentioned above indicates the sophistication of court life during the Dvaravati period. Other scenes illustrate servants bearing objects, musicians and dancers, and a group of prisoners being kicked by their guard (Fig. 20).

Fig. 20: Stucco figure showing a group of prisoners being kicked by their guard, from Ku Bua, Ratchaburi Province.

LANGUAGES

Available inscriptions indicate that the literate people of the Dvaravati period were familiar with three languages, Sanskrit, Pali, and Old Mon. The two Indian languages had spread throughout most of South-East Asia at that time. They were official, scholarly, and religious languages, and probably used in everyday speech.

CONCEPTS OF STATE AND KINGSHIP

The coinage of Dvaravati confirms that some Indian concepts of state and kingship were accepted by the Dvaravati rulers. Inscribed silver coins from the main Dvaravati sites such as Nakhon Pathom, U-Thong, Ku Bua, Ku Muang, Brahma-tin, Dong Khon and U Ta-Pao, indicate kingship existed during the Dvaravati times. On the obverse of each coin are engraved Indian symbols of fertility and prosperity, such as *purnaghata*, and the cow or deer with offspring. On the reverse the words *sridvaravatisvarapunya* are inscribed. We also have supporting evidence from a large number of uninscribed silver coins distributed over a wide area, which bear symbols such as the rising sun or *sankha* and *srivatsa*, as stated above. These have been found throughout the Dvaravati territories and in contemporary cities influenced by Indian civilization from Burma to the lower Mekong Valley.

These coins were issued by Dvaravati kings, as confirmed by the findings of stone moulds bearing the *sankha* symbol from U-Thong and Chansen, and a clay mould bearing the sun symbol from U-Thong.[29] The kings aspired to expand their economy and to enhance their position at the head of it. This hypothesis is confirmed by the Chinese sources. The description of the Dvaravati kingdom of Tung-tien, compiled by Tu Yu (a Chinese historian) in the late eighth century, records that here, if a man casts silver coins without permission, his arm is to be cut-off.[30]

Although the Dvaravati kings were devout Buddhists, it is believed that they were exalted far above ordinary mortals through the magical power of the *Rajasuya*—royal consecration—which imbued the king with divine power. Some objects meant for ritual purposes have been discovered, such as stone tablets or trays depicting a series of royal insignia including *camara* (flywhisks), *sankha*, *vajra* (thunderbolts), *valvijani* (fans), *ankusa* (elephant goads) and *chhatra* (umbrellas). These stone tablets are reported from Nakhon Pathom[31] and from Dong Khon, Chainat Province.[32] It is presumed that the bone dice from Nern Makok, Lopburi Province, is another kind of ritual object (Fig. 21). According to the *Satapatha Brahmana,* these objects might have been used in a series of rituals performed during the *Rajasuya* ceremony.[33] These rituals were:

(a)

(b)

Fig. 21: A bone dice from Nern Makok, Lopburi Province.

1. Offerings to household deities;
2. Sprinkling ceremony (*abhisecaneya*);
3. The king's symbolic walk towards the various quarters, as an indication of his universal rule;
4. Treading upon the tiger's skin, thus gaining the strength of the tiger;
5. Enthronement;
6. A mimic cow raid, symbolizing the king as the war leader of pastoral people;
7. Narration by priest of the *Sunhsepa* legend of the *Aitareya Brahmana,* which reflects the structure of class society;
8. The game of dice—the eighth item of the *Rajasuya*—in which the king participates, to symbolize the division of food.

The stone tablets or trays which depict a series of royal insignia with a small circular depression in the middle might have been receptacles for holding a pot of water to be used in rituals such as the sprinkling ceremony (*abhisecaniya*), the second item mentioned in the *Rajasuya.* And the bone dice might have been used in the ritual game of dice, the eighth item mentioned in the *Rajasuya.*

According to Buddhist tradition, the Dvaravati kings could also be regarded Universal Emperors or *Cakravartin*, as recorded in the *Cakkavattisihanada Sutta.*[34]

Just as Buddha appears from time to time in the cosmic cycle, heralded by auspicious omens and endowed with favourable signs, to lead all living beings along the road to enlightenment, so does a Universal Emperor appear, to conquer all *Jambudvipa* and rule prosperously and righteously.

This indicates that the *cakra* or wheel (symbol of sovereignty) of the state chariot rolls everywhere without obstruction. It is believed that the Mauryas developed the concept of *Cakravartin,* which was incorporated into Buddhist tradition. A relief from the stupa of Jaggayyapeta (*c.* 200–100 BC) depicts the *Cakravartin* scene with the Emperor in the centre; on his right is the wheel, symbolizing the Universal Empire; on his left are the Chief Queen, the Chief Minister, and the Crown Prince; and at his feet are the imperial elephant and horse.[35]

Stone *dharmacakras* that symbolize the universal empire, and Buddha images and Buddhist monuments of the typical Dvaravati

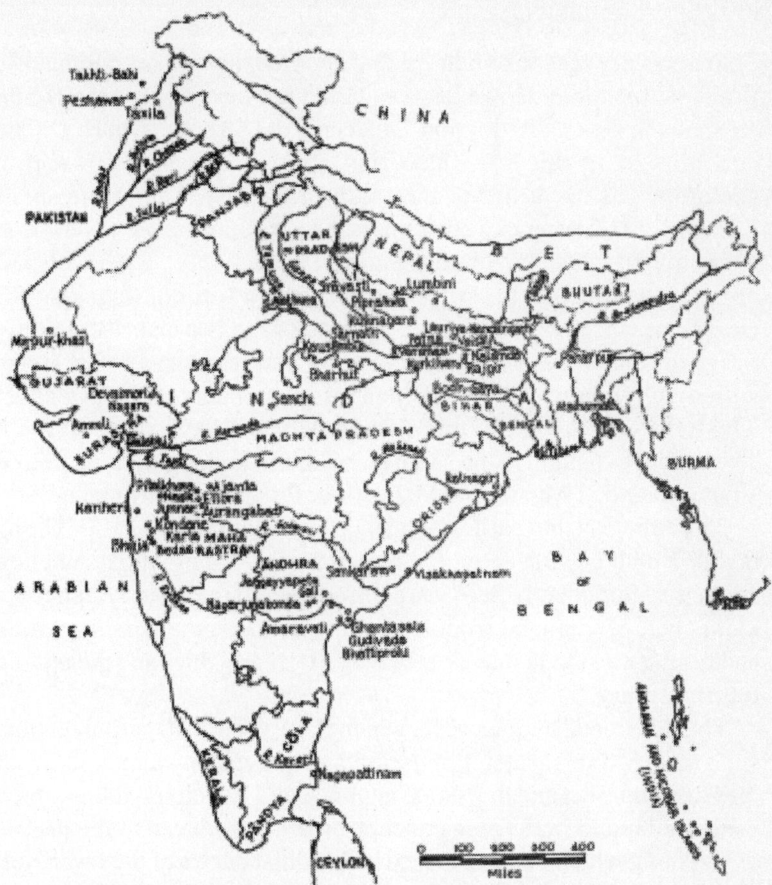

Map 4: The remains of Buddhist sites in India.

style have been discovered at the main Dvaravati sites of Central Thailand and at the other sites where Dvaravati culture spread. These include the northern region of Haripunjaya,[36] the north-eastern region at Muang Sema, Fa Daed, and Na Dune;[37] and the southern region such as Chaiya and Yarang.[38] These examples indicate that the Dvaravati kings had followed the Buddhist concept as recorded in the *Cakkavattisihanada Sutta* and practised by King Asoka. The Dvaravati kings tried to emulate Asoka in establishing *dharma* and *dharma-vijaya* in foreign regions, and thus they may be regarded as *digvijayins*, conquerors of all the four quarters.

RELIGIOUS BELIEFS (MAP 4)

There is every reason to believe that Dvaravati was a predominantly Buddhist kingdom. However, we should not lose sight of the Hindu elements in Dvaravati religion, especially at U-Thong, where a stone *mukhalinga* in the Pre-Angkorian style of the seventh-eighth centuries was unearthed to the south of the city. The existence of Saivism at U-Thong is well supported by a copper-plate inscription of about 650 which mentions the gift of a jewel litter, a parasol, and musical instruments to the *Amratakesvara* (a form of linga) by Sri Harsavarman, grandson of the king Sri Isanavarman.[39] Not only Saivism, but traces of Vaisnavism are also evident in two stelae with rough figures of Visnu in high relief, probably in Pallava style, which have been kept in the U-Thong *San Chao* or spirit shrine.[40] They seem to belong to the same group of the Pallava-derived mitred Visnus found at Muang Sri Mahosot in Prachinburi Province.[41]

Nevertheless, the earliest evidence of religious belief at U-Thong is still Buddhist. Based on the remains at U-Thong, most scholars agree that Buddhist beliefs were introduced to the Dvaravati people in this part of Thailand from Nagarjunakonda on the Krishna which had been under the Ikshavakus between the early third and the middle fourth century.[42]

The different Buddhist sects which flourished at Nagarjunakonda, such as the Mahisasaka, Bahusrutiya, Chaityakas which split from the Hinayana sect and the Mahasanghika, and Lokottaravadins which were inclined to Mahayana concepts, were introduced to the people of U-Thong which became the early Buddhist centre of the Dvaravati kingdom by the fourth century, if not earlier. The influence of different Buddhist sects from Nagarjunakonda can be seen in the architectural and sculptural remains left there, and of the Dvaravati sites. As they established Buddhist symbols such as the stone *dharmacakra* on a pillar found near Stupa 11 at U-Thong,[43] they worshipped Buddha images: we have many examples of bronze and stone images from the main Dvaravati sites (Figs 22, 23). They also believed in stupa worship. A large number of small stupas have been constructed within and beyond the moated sites, such as U-Thong, Ku Bua, and Muang Bon. Most of them were similar in plan, having a square brick stupa base with stairways on each face. And it is noticed that the devout Buddhists preferred constructing

Fig. 22: Standing Buddha (bronze) from U-Thong, Supanburi Province.

Fig. 23: Seated Buddha under Naga (stone), from Dong Sri Mahabodhi, Prachinburi Province.

Mahachaityas in the centre of the important cities such as Chula Paton at Nakhon Pathom, Wat Klong at Ku Bua, and Kao Klang Nai at Sri Thep.[44]

We also learn from inscriptions and from Buddhist remains in the main Dvaravati sites that Dvaravati Buddhism was influenced not only from the Krishna-Godavari Valleys, but also from Buddhist centres in other parts of India. There is, for instance, evidence to show that the religious beliefs of the Hinayana Sammitiya sect, held by the Buddhists of western India at Valabhi (Gujarat), under the patronage of the Saka-Kshatrapas (*c*. AD 200–400), and the Maitrakas (*c*. AD 400–800) had much influence on Dvaravati Buddhism.

The Dvaravati people not only constructed a large number of stupas, mahastupas, and Buddha images, they also produced a large number of religious objects. Archaeologists have discovered votive stupas, terracotta tablets, votive tablets, terracotta begging bowls inscribed in Pali with the words *Ye Dhamma*. The stone *Dharma-cakras*, interestingly, were inscribed in Pali with *Pratityasamutpada-sutra*, that teaching considered as of paramount importance by the Buddhists of Valabhi in the sixth and seventh centuries. The Chinese pilgrim I-tsing did not fail to notice this widely prevalent practice. According to his record, when Indian people made images and *chaityas* of gold, silver, copper, iron, earth, lacquer, bricks and stone, they put in the images and *chaiyas* two kinds of *sariras* relics: those of the Great Teacher, and the *gatha* of the Chain of Causation (*Pratitya-samutpada-sutra*). The merits derived from enshrining the two kinds of *sarira* were supposedly enormous. The fact that the Gatha was called *sarira* shows that it had assumed the sanctity of a relic of the Buddha.[45] The sculptural art of Dvaravati came under the influence of Buddhism from centres flourishing in the northern and eastern regions and in the Deccan. From Sarnath in the north, a wheel flanked by two deer symbolizing the First Sermon in the Deer Park become the accepted emblem of the seals of almost all the *mahaviharas* of India,[46] and this was considered to be of paramount importance by the Dvaravati people. Stone dharmacakras and deer images have been reported from most of the main Dvaravati sites. The sculptural art of Dvaravati was also influenced by Mahayana Buddhism from the Deccan under the patronage of the Gupta and the Vakataka rulers (*c*. 300–600), while the art of the Deccan caves at Ajanta, Karle, and Kanheri was imitated by Dvaravati artists: Thus the colossal images of Buddha seated in *pralambapada-asana*, reliefs of preaching Buddha, and depictions of the Great Miracle at Sravasti.[47] A number of colossal images of Buddha are recorded at Dvaravati sites such as the quartzite statues of Wat Pra Men, Nakhon Pathom[48] (Fig. 24) and the relief carving of the Buddha in the Khao Ngu cave, Ratchaburi Province. Terracotta votive tablets depict the Buddha giving a discourse on the True Doctrine. The Lotus Sutra, and the Great Miracle of Sravasti as described in the *Divyavadana*[49] have also been made by the Dvaravati artists.[50]

A number of stone bas-reliefs are known from Nakhon Pathom, Sri Thep, Sab Champa and some other sites.[51] Each of them depicts a curious bird vehicle on which the Buddha and his two attendants are standing (Fig. 25). The vehicle (*vahana*) is labelled *vanaspati*, a combination of the characteristics of *hamsa, garuda* and bull vehicles

Fig. 24: Colossal image of seated Buddha (stone) from Wat Phra Men, Nakhon Pathom.

Fig. 25: Stone bas-relief depicting the Buddha and his two attendants are standing on the curious bird vehicle, from Nakhon Pathom.

Fig. 26: Terracotta medallion depicting Gaja-Laksmi and Kubera, from Muang Chansen, Nakhon Sawan Province.

Fig. 27: A headless man with a monkey (terracotta), from U-Thong, Supanburi Province.

Fig. 28: Lion amulet (terracotta), from Nakhon Pathom.

of Brahma, Visnu, and Siva. This combination seems to be a peculiarly Dvaravati conception which was undoubtedly influenced by the Vajrayana school of Mahayana Tantra flourishing in north-eastern India under the patronage of the Pala kings (*c.* 800–1200). The Vajrayanists always displayed a great hatred towards the Hindu gods who were usually shown as the favourite vehicles of the Buddhist gods.

Last, we should mention the amulets that were prevalent in Dvaravati times. The round terracotta medallions found at the main Dvaravati sites depicting Gaja-Laksmi (Fig. 26) were used to ward off misfortunes and to bestow wealth from trade. Human-shaped amulets were quite popular. A number of headless human figurines, both male and female, particularly a headless man with a monkey (Fig. 27) have been reported from the main Dvaravati sites.[52] However, it seems that lion amulets (Fig. 28) were most popular. The lion symbolizes not only power but also the Buddha's status as Sakya Simha, the lion of the Sakya race.

NOTES

1. S. Beal, *Buddhist Records of the Western World/Translated from the Chinese of Hiuen Tsiang (A.D. 629)*, Delhi: Oriental Books Reprint Corporation, 1969; Takakusu, J (tr.), *A Record of the Buddhist Religion as Practised in India and the Malay Archipelago (A.D. 371–695) by I. Tsing*, 2nd Indian edn., New Delhi: Munshiram Manoharlal, 1982.
2. J.J. Boeles, 'The King of Sri Dvaravati and His Regalia', *JSS*, 52, 1 (April. 1964): 99–114.
3. S. Pou, and P.N. Jenner, 'Proto-Indonesian and Mon-Khmer', *Asian Perspectives*, XVII, 2 (1974): 112–24.
4. P. Vanasin, and Th. Supajanya, *Ancient Cities on the Former Coastline in the Central Plain of Thailand: The Study of Sites and Geographical Corelation*, Bangkok: Chulalongkorn University Press, 1980 (in Thai).
5. P. Dupont, *L'Archeologie Mon de Dvaravati*, Paris: Ecole Francaise d'Extreme-Orient. 1959.
6. J.J. Boeles, loc. cit.
7. G. Coedès, 'Les E'tats Hindouise's d'Indochine et Indonesie', Paris, 1964, p. 93.
8. J. Chongkol, *National Museum Bangkok*, Bangkok: Siwaporn, 1984 (in Thai); Ph. Indrawooth, 'Amulets for Merchants', *Archaeology Journal*, Special Issue: to commemorate its 30th Anniversary (in Thai).
9. Dh. Yupho, *Quartzite Buddha Images of the Dvaravati Period*, Bangkok: Siwaporn Printing (in Thai).
10. G. Coedes, 'Une Roue de la Loi avec inscription en Pali provenant du site de Pra Pathom', *Artibus Asiae* 19 (1956): 221–6.
11. Ph. Indrawooth, *The Excavation at the Ancient Town of Nakhon Pathom, Tambon Phra Praton, Amphoe Muang, Changwat Nakhon Pathom*, Nakhon Pathom: Silpakorn University Press (in Thai).
12. Ph. Indrawoth, *Report on the Excavation at Muang Fa Daed Song Yang Kamalasai District, Kalasin Province*, Nakhon Pathom: Silpakorn University Press, 2001, p. 69.
13. T.N. Roy, *The Ganges Civilization*, New Delhi, 1983, Chapters 2, and 4.
14. H.G. Quaritch Wales, 'Muang Bon: A Town of Northern Dvaravati', *JSS* 53, 1 (January 1965): 1–7.
15. H.G. Quaritch Wales, *The Exploration of Sri Deva: An Ancient Indian City in Indochina*, Reprinted from Indian Art and Letters, vol. X, 2, London: The India Society, 1937: 61–99.
16. Ph. Indrawooth, S., Krabuansang, S. and P. Narkwake, 'Muang Fa Daed Song Yang: New Archaeological Evidence', in *Recentes Recherches en Archeologie en Thailande: Deuxieme Symposium Fronco-Thai*, Bongkok: Silpakorn University, 98-111.
17. T. Amatayakul, *Changwat Suphan Buri*, Bangkok: Charoenrat Printing Press, 1970, pp. 34–37 (in Thai).

18. P. Gutman, 'The Ancient Coinage of Southeast Asia', *JSS* 66, 1 (1948): 8–12.
19. P. Jiachanphong, 'Terracotta Seals from Khok Chanson', in Chansen: *A Social and Cultural History*, Bangkok: Ruen Kaew Printing House, 1996, 168–89 (in Thai).
20. Ph. Indrawooth, *The Excavation at the Ancient Town of Nakhon Pathom*, loc. cit.
21. T.N. Roy, *The Ganges Civilization*, loc. cit.
22. P. Pisnupong, ed., *Report on the Excavation of the Sra Morakot Monuments*, Bangkok: Samaphan Printing, 1991 (in Thai).
23. S. Rattanakun, *Archaeology of Muang Ku Bua*, Bangkok: Fine Arts Department, 1992.
24. Ph. Indrawooth, *Index Pottery of Dvaravati Period*, Bangkok: Thai I.E. Printing Group. 1985; R.C. Singh, R.C. Prasad 'Spouted Vessels in India', in B.P. Singh (ed.), *Potteries in Ancient India*, Patna: Patna University, 1969, pp. 275–84.
25. G. Coedès, 'Excavation at Pong Tuk', *Journal of the Siam Society*, vol. XXI, Part 3, 1928, pp. 195-209.
26. M.N. Despande, 'Roman Potteries in India', in B.P. Singh. ed., *Potteries in Ancient India*, loc. cit. pp. 275-84.
27. D.P.S. Peacock, *Pottery in the Roman World: An Ethnoarchaeological Approach*, London and New York: Longman, 1982; K. Greene, *Roman Pottery*, London: British Museum Press, 1992.
28. Rattanakun, 1992, *Archaeology of Muang Ku Bua*, loc. cit.
29. Bhumathon, 'Dvaravati Uninscribed Coins Found at Lopburi', *Silpakorn Journal*, 28, 5 (1984): 55–63 (in Thai).
30. T. Yamamoto, 'East Asian Historical Sources for Dvaravati Studies', *Proceedings: Seventh IAHA Conference*, Bangkok, August 1977, Bangkok: Chulalongkorn University Press House, pp. 1137–50.
31. J.J. Boeles, 'The King of Sri Dvaravati', loc. cit.
32. B. Bhumadhon, *The Archaeology of Muang Dong Khon*, Bangkok: Amarin Printing and Publishing Public Company, 1987 (in Thai).
33. N.N. Bhattacharyya, *Ancient Indian Rituals and Their Social Contents*, London: Curzon Press, 1975.
34. T.W. Rhys Davids (tr.), *Dialogues of the Buddha*, London: Luzac and Company, 1656, pp. 92–3.
35. B. Rowland, *The Art and Architecture of India (Hindu-Buddhist-Jain)*, London: Penguin, 1953, Pl. 16 (A).
36. Ph. Indrawooth, 'The study of ancient civilization from archaeological evidence in Lumphun prior to the 19th century B.E.', *Archaeology Journal*, Special Issue: to commemorate its 40th Anniversary: 7–44 (in Thai).
37. Fine Arts Department, *The Survey and Excavation at Muang Fa Daed* Song Yang, Amphoe Komalasai, Changwat Kalasin, 1967–68, Bangkok,

1968; Veeraprasert, M., 'Tablettes Votives Bouddhiques de la Periode de Dvaravati decouvertes a Nadun, Mahasarakham', in *Premier Symposium Franco-Thai, La Thailande-des debuts de son Histoire au XV eme siecle* (18-20 Juillet 1988), 124–9.

38. P. Krairiksh, *Art in Peninsula Thailand Prior to the Fourteenth Century A.D.*, Bangkok: Amarin Printing Group, 1980, pl. 26.
39. G. Coedès, 'Nouvelles donnes epigraphiques sur l'histoire de l'Indochinine Centrale', *Journal Asiatiques*, CXLVI (1658): 125–42.
40. E. L. de, Lajonquiere, 'Le domaine archeologique du Siam', *BCAI* (1909): 188–262.
41. Fine Arts Department, *History and Archaeology of Sri Mahosot*, Bangkok: Samaphan Printing, 1992.
42. G. Boisselier, 'U-Thong et son importance pour l'histoire de Thailande', *Silpakorn Journal*, 9, 1 (1965): 27–30.
43. S. Rattanakun, *Report on the Excavation at Muang U-Thong*, Fine Arts Department, 1966.
44. W. Tankittikorn, *The Settlement Before Muang Sri Thep*, Bangkok: Future Press, 1991 (in Thai).
45. J. Takakusu (tr.), *A Record of the Buddhist*, loc. cit.
46. D. Mitra, *Buddhist Monuments*, Calcutta: Sahitya Samsad, 1971, Part II pp. 21–3.
47. D. Mitra, *Ajanta*, Calcutta: Archaeological Survey of India, Government of India, 1966: pl. XIV; C.K. Owen, *Buddhist Cave Temples of India*, Bombay: D.B. Taraporevala, 1975, pls. 8 and 38.
48. Dh. Yupho, *Quartzite Buddha Images of the Dvaravati Period*, Bangkok: Siwaporn Printing (in Thai).
49. G. Coedès, *Recueil des Inscriptions du Siam*, Part II, Bangkok, 1929.
50. H. Kern, (tr.), *The Saddharma-Pundarika or the Lotus of the True Law*, The Sacred Books of the East Series, vol. XXI, Delhi: Motilal Banarsidass, 1974.
51. J.K. Nariman, *Literary History of Sanskrit Buddhism*, Delhi, 1972, Chapter VI, pp. 45–63.
52. N. Sirisrap, 'Dvaravati Terracotta Votive Tablets at Nakhon Pathom', M.A. Thesis, Faculty of Archaeology, Silpakorn University, 1981.

An Exploration of the Advent of Buddhism in Thailand

SIYARAM MISHRA HALDHAR

Archaeological finds at Pongtuk and Phra Pathom confirm that Buddhism flourished in Thailand from a very early period. However, traditionally, it is believed that Buddhism was introduced here during the reign of Emperor Asoka. There is archaeological evidence of the prevalence of Hinayana in ancient Dvāravatī (covering included large areas of modern Thailand) from the sixth century. It is conjuctured that the Thai people received the Buddhist faith either from Mön people to the west Thailand or from the kingdom or Sri Dhammarāja (modern Ligor) in Malay peninsula: Theravāda was flourishing in both these regions.

Dvāravati has flourishing Mön kingdom whose political influence extended as far as Haripuñjaya (modern Lampun province) in northern Thailand. A Mön inscription found at Kaslo (Lopburi) which may be dated to the sixth-seventh century appears to be palaeographically closely related to the Pallava script of south India, where Theravāda Buddhism had flourished during the fourth and fifth centuries. Architectural and sculptural remains from the sixth century onwards indicated that Theravāda Buddhism flourished in the lower Menam valley. The Haripuñjaya kingdom of the upper Menam valley was an important power in northern Thailand. It is said that the king of Lopburi sent his daughter Cammādevi to become the ruler of Haripuñjaya. She came to Haripuñjaya, in the second half of the seventh century, with soldiers and 500 *mahatheras* well-versed in the *Tipitaka*. Towards the thirteenth century the Haripuñjaya kingdom had become a great centre of Mön culture and it was also a centre of Theravāda Buddhism. The several inscriptions discovered here are all in the Mön language mixed with Pāli, and hint at the prevalence of Theravāda in the upper Menam valley. Jetavane was one of the most important monasteries in Haripuñjaya: it housed over 100 novices.

The Thais made themselves masters of Siam and Laos towards the middle of the thirteenth century and put an end to the political supermacy of the Cambodians over them. The establishment of Sukhothai/Sukhodaya as the capital of the Thai Kingdom after AD 1250 is an important event in political history and also in the history of Buddhism in Thailand. Now a regular religious and cultural intercourse with Sri Lanka largely via Siridhammanaja in the Malay Peninsula and Myammar, began. King Rocaraja of Sukhothai was the first king to establish direct contact with Sri Lanka around the second half of the thirteenth century. At his request Sukhothai received its first Buddha image from Sri Lanka. Under the influence of the Thai rulers, Buddhism of the Theravāda school and the Pāli language flourished all over Thailand and Laos.

According to Jinkālamāli, the Sinhalese Buddhist saṅgha was established during the reigns of Dhammarāja of Sukhothai and Lothai (1317–47). According to Jinatatiālā, a famous Sri Lanka Mahāthera named Udumbara Mahāsāmī arrived in the Ramañña where a Siamese monk, Name Sumona, from Sukhothai received the *upasampadā* (ordination) and also studied the religious text under him. At the request of Lothai, Udumbara Mahāsāmī sent the Elder Simana to established the Sinhalse form of the monastic discipline. The *Mūlsānsa* also testifies the Jinakālamāli version of the statement. Lo Thai built many Buddhapādas (replicas of the foot print of the Buddha) in imitation of that worshipped in Sri Lanka on the summit of Samantakūta. At that time a Thai prince donned the robe and visited India and Sri Lanka and brought back relics. After returning he not only restored but also enlarged that Wat Mahādhātu of Sukhothai. Lemay observes the art of these buildings, perhaps executed in part by workers brought from Sri Lanka.

Kilanā, the king of Nabbisipura requested there Udumbara Mahāsāmī to send to him a Thera who could perform all religious acts, and Ānanda Thera was sent to Nabbisipura. On the advice of Ānanda Thera, the king requested the king of Sukhothai to invite the elder Sumana to his kingdom.

The king Luthāi/Lü Thai who ascended the throne in AD 1347 was a man of culture and devoted his time to the propagation of Buddhism. He built a large number of Buddhist centres and temples. He himself had embraced the life of a Buddhist monk. About 1361 he sent some learned monks and scholars to Sri Lanka and persuaded the great monk called Mahāsāmī Saṇgha Rāja to come to Thailand Under his active guidance and encouragement as well as the vigorous endeavour the king, Buddhism and Pāli literature obtained a firm footing. Buddhism spread to a number of Hinduized states. One of his inscriptions, which gives him the title Sri Sūnyavamsa Rāma Mahādharam Rājadhirāja, provides vivid details of the welcome accorded to a hierarch from Sri Lanka who was invited to Thailand to reorganize the religious institutions there. This resulted in Sukhothai becoming a great centre of Buddhist studies in the middle of the fifteenth century. The Nagar Jum (one of the districts in modern Kamphaeng Phet in central Thailand) inscription dated 1357 states that a sacred and authentic relic of the Buddha was brought to Thailand from Sri Lanka and was installed with great solemnity by the king at Nagar Jum. Two inscriptions found at Sukhothai refer to the invitation sent by King Luthāi to Mahāsāmī Sanghraja of Sri Lanka, his installation at the monastery of the mango grove, and the ordaining of King Luthāi. During the reign of Luthāi, a Siamese monk called Mahāthera Sriraddhāraja Cūlāmuni Sriratanalankādīpa Mahāsāmī visited Sri Lanka, and having obtained two sacred relics, returned to Thailand along with several Sri Lankan laymen. The latter are said to have taken residence in five villages in Thailand. Thus we know that in medieval times the Buddhists of Thailand turned to Sri Lanka for religious inspiration.

In the middle of the fourteenth century the new kingdom of Ayutthiya became the centre of political power. The rulers of this dynasty patronized cultural and religious intercourse with Sri Lanka. There is sufficient reason to believe that strong religious ties existed between the two countries and the Sinhalese sangha played an important role in Thailand. Boromrāja of Paramarāja I (1370–88) built the Lankārāma and during the reign Dhammakitti thera of Ayutthiya came to Sri Lanka to study under Dhammapitti Mahāsāmī.

Tissarāja (1401 to 1442) and his son Tilakarāja/Tilakaraja (1442–87) played a significant part in the development of Buddhism in northern Thailand. His reign is often described as the golden period of painting, literature, and religion in Nabbisipura. The king himself is said to have entered the sangha in 1447 for some time, and with the permission of his teacher he assumed office again as king.

The elder Somacitta established the Sinhalese sangha in the Khemaraṭṭha, the Khema kingdom of the Shan, in 1448. The king built one Uposata hall at the Rattavanamahāvihāra (Wat Pa Daeng Lung) in 1451 and it was sanctioned as a Simā. In 1445 a seedling grown from a branch of the Mahābodhi at Anuradhapura was planted by King Tilakarāja in the premises of Wat Budhārāma Mahāvihāra at Nabbisipura Chieng Mai, by the order of Sri Lalagotta. The king's General built the Rajakūta (Phrachedi Luang) near Nabbisipura. A Buddha image named Ratanapatmā was also installed in the Rajakūta. The Jinakālamāli, which give the story of the images, relates that this was originally fashioned by king Milinda according to the advice of Thera Nāgasena and after some time was brought to Sri Lanka. King Anurddha of Pagan is said to have taken it from Sri Lanka to Myanmar. In turn, the images was taken to various cities in Cambodia and Thailand, until in the reign of Tilakarāja, it found its final resting place at Chieng Mai. This statue is reckoned as the most important image in Thailand, and at present it rests in the royal chapel of the Cakkri grand place in Bangkok. The relic brought by Mahā Dhammagambhīra was also deposited in this shrine in the year 1487. King Tilakarāja had convened a grand council in the Mahābodhi Arāma at Nabissipura in 1475 for revising the Pāli scriptures.

The Emperor Jāmerāgye (Chieng Rai) ascended the throne of Nabbisipura in 1487. He built Tapodārāma (Wat Pampung). He purified a Khaṇdasimā at the Upari Arāma Monster (Wat Bon) in northern Thailand in about 1495. King Tikalapanattu (1495–1525) is regarded as one of the greatest kings of Thailand. He contributed significantly to the development of Buddhism, building many temples. In 1497 he built Pubbārāma. He also built the Mahādhātu Cetiya at Haripuñjaya with a stone wall constructed around the city for its safety.

Bayinnaung, the Myanmarese king of Pegu, captured most of Thailand during the second half of the sixteenth century. He also worked for the progress of Buddhism. King Naresuen ascended the throne of Ayutthiya in AD 1590 and expelled the Myanmarese from Thailand and captured parts of Cambodia.

Christianity made its entry into Thailand during the reign of King Narai (1656–88). The eighteenth century witnessed revival in Thailand's religious intercourse with Sri Lanka. King Mahā

Dhammarāja II (Boromokot) ascended the throne of Ayutthiya in 1732 and constructed many monasteries throughout his kingdom. Ayutthiya became a great centre of Buddhism. Religious missions from Sri Lanka came there to get help and assistance from Thai monks. Thus, it is interesting to note that although Thailand was deeply influenced by Sri Lanka in respect of its religion, it repayed its debt in some measure when in about 1750 the king of Sri Lanka sent a messenger to the king of Thailand and the latter sent golden and silver images of the Buddha, copies of sacred texts, and ten monks under the leadership of Upāli Mahāthera.

In 1767, Myanmar invaded Ayutthiya and destroyed most of it. The ruler of Thailand shifted his capital to Bangkok. General Cakkri, who was known as Ram I (1782-1809), was the founder of the present reigning dynasty at Bangkok. Buddhism continues to flourish under the patronage of the rulers of this dynasty.

SELECT BIBLIOGRAPHY

Briggs, I.P., The *Ancient Khmer Empire*, Philadelphia, 1951.

Buddhadata Mahathera, A.P. (ed.), *Jinkālamāli*, London: PTS, 1962.

Cady, J.F., *Thailand, Burma, Laos and Cambodia*, 1966.

Coedès, G., *The Making of South-East Asia*, tr. from French by H. M. Wright, London, 1966.

Conze, E., *A Short History of Buddhism*, Oxford, 1960.

Dult, N., *Early Monastic Buddhism*, Calcutta, 1941.

Gokhale, G.G., 'Early Buddhism and the Urban Revolution', *The Journal of the International Association of Buddhist Studies*, vol. 5 (2), 1987, 7-22.

Haldhar, S.M., *Buddhism in Myanmar and Thailand*, Delhi: Om Publications, 2003.

———, 'A Study of Time and Place of Dhamma Cakkappavattana', *Buddhist Studies*, vol. XXVI, February 2005, pp. 96–103.

———, 'An Exploration of Facts of Advent of Buddhism in Myanmar', *Buddhist Studies*, vol. XXVII, March 2005, pp. 58–64.

Hall, D.G.E., *A History of South-East Asia*, New York, 1970.

Hazra, K.L., *History of Theravāda Buddhism in South-East Asia*, Delhi, 1982.

———, *The Buddhist Annals and Chronicles of South-East Asia*, Delhi, 1986.

Le May, Reginald, *A Concise History of Buddhist Art in Siam*, Cambridge: PWD, 1938.

Lester, Robert, *Theravāda Buddhism in South-East Asia*, Ann Arbor, 1973.

Sarao, K.T.S. (ed), *A Textbook of History of Thervada Buddhism*, Department of Buddhist Studies, Delhi University, 1915.

Smith, Bardwell L., *Religion and Legitimation of Power in Thailand*, Laos and Burma, Chambersburg, 1978.

Wales, H.G., *Dvāravati: The Earliest Kingdom of Siam 6th to 11th Century AD*, London: Quartich, 1969.

Syncretism and Thai Buddhism

BACHCHAN KUMAR

The state religion of Thailand is Theravada Buddhism. The most important features of traditional Theravada Buddhism are the use of Pali as a sacred language and the acceptance of the Pali Buddhist Canon, the *Tripitaka*, as the scripture. In Thai Buddhism, however, *Tripitakas* are not directly relevant to religious belief and practices. Other religious practices have also influenced the religious code of conduct of Thai people. In this paper, I propose to examine syncretism in Thai Buddhism to discuss the nature and basic features of Buddhism in Thailand.

Before coming to Thai Buddhism, it would be pertinent to analyse the term syncretism. This term usually refers to connections of a special kind between languages, cultures, or religions. In the history of religions, a special effort has been made to give the term a more precise meaning. In modern times a study on syncretism was first made by Richard Reitzenstein and H.H. Schaeder in their book entitled *Classic Studien zum antiken Synkretismus aus Iran und Griechenland*, Leipzig, 1926. Investigations continued in a series of symposia: *Syncretism: Based on Papers Read at the Symposium on Cultural Contact, Meeting on Religious Syncretism Held at Abo on the 8–10 September 1966*, edited by Sven S. Hartman, Stockholm, 1969; Les syncretismes dans les religions grecque et romaine; colloque de Strasbourg, 9–11 June 1971, Paris, 1973; *Synkretismus im syrisch-persischen Kulturgebiet: Bericht uber ein Symposion in Reinhausen bei Gottingen in der Zeit 4–8 October 1971*, edited by Albrecht Dietrich, Gottingen, 1975; *Les syncretismes dans les religions de l'antiquite: Colloque de Besancon, 22–23 October 1973*, edited by Francoise Dunand and Pierre L. Leveque, Leiden, 1975; and *Religious Syncretism in Antiquity: Essays in Conversation with Geo Widengren*, edited by Birger A Pearson, Missoula, 1975. A recent approach has been made in Ulrich Berner's *Untersuchungen zur Vewendung des Synkretismus-Begriffes*, Wiesbaden, 1982.

The Greek term *sygkretismos* was first used by Plutarch (AD 46-120). It is derived from the verb *sygkretizo* probably based on *sygkreos*, the Ionian form of *sugkratos* which means mixed together.[1] There may be two interpretations of syncretism in the socio-philosophical sphere: static and dynamic. In the first case, the concept is used to indicate a situation where certain components or traits have been integrated with one another, When used in the diachronic context the term means a trend, stages of development extending over a period of time, which results in syncretism. In German, *Mischerei*, unlike *Mischung* (mixture, blending), has negative overtones and in fact users regarded the phenomenon of syncretism as an unprincipled abandonment of the faith of the fathers, even though it was at the same time a necessary transitional stage in the history of religions. Later, the word came to be used mostly without negative overtones, but it continued to be applied in all sorts of ways. This word now means 'to grow together in a natural way'.

In different epochs of human civilization, readjustments of political and social relationships, sometimes arising from the contact or the clash of various cultures and civilizations, had led to the fusion of ideas, practices, and beliefs. It has taken the shape of either one group accepting the principles of another or amalgamation into a 'more cosmopolitan and less polytheistic' phenomenon. In the philosophy of religion, the term 'syncretism' is used for the identification of diverse deities and the combination or fusion of their cults. One of the results of syncretism in religions is a sense of tolerance and sympathy. People who are ready to borrow from other religions are clearly not about to condemn them. In general, syncretism tends to induce a belief in pantheism. Since the inception of Thai society, its religion interacted with various Buddhist and non-Buddhists elements, which gave it much complexity in nature and form. Some scholars, however, distinguish three components in Thai Buddhism: Buddhism, Brahmanism, and the cult of ancestors or spirit worship.

ORIGIN AND DEVELOPMENT OF THERAVADA BUDDHISM

Tradition places the date of the introduction of Buddhism in Thailand as early as the time of the Buddha himself and by the Buddha himself.

It is a common belief in Thailand, even now, that the Buddha visited the country at least once and on that occasion impressed his footprint on a hill in the present-day Saraburi about 150 km north of Bangkok. This particular footprint was discovered by King Sri Dharmaraja well over two thousand years after the Master's death, in AD 1602.[2] According to popular belief, the Buddha not only visited Thailand but actually attained *Mahaparinirvana* at Pra Ten, a little to the north of Pra Pathom (Nakhon Pathom) on a spot marked by a slab of rock under great trees.[3]

This appears to be a legend devoid of historical content. The Sri Lankan and Burmese traditions also claim, in a similar manner, visits by the master to their respective Lands. Because of his visit, people in those countries were converted to the teachings of Buddha, they built monuments to commemorate the occasion and to perpetuate the memory of his visits. Such beliefs are indicators of how effectively the teachings of Buddha had permeated the life of the people of South-East Asia.

Further, the spread of Buddhism to these countries was at first initiated by Emperor Asoka, who reigned during the third century BC. On a decision taken at the Third Buddhist Council at Pataliputra Asoka sent missionaries to foreign countries. One of the nine missions mentioned in the Sri Lankan chronicles was led by Sona and Uttara and went to Suvarnabhumi, the land of gold.

Scholars have different opinions regarding the location of Suvarnabhumi. Majumdar opines that Burma, the Malay Peninsula and Sumatra constitute Suvarnabhumi.[4] In the opinion of Coedès, Suvarnabhumi in the Pali texts or Suvarnakundya (the wall of the Gold) in Sanskrit correspond to lower Burma and the Malaya peninsula.[5] The Burmese historians identify the Land of Gold as Thaton, lower Burma, to the West of Rangoon, near the Thai northern frontier. This view is also supported by some European scholars.[6] According to them, Asoka's mission was sent to Thaton.

The Burmese view is based on indigenous chronicles, which lack historical exactitude. Prince Damrong Rajanubhab who is rightly called the 'father of Thai history', identifies the city of Nakhon Pathom (Nagara Pathame—the first city) in Thailand. The archaeological evidence, however, support Damrong's view. M.C. Subhadradis Diskul[7] states that votive tablets and some silver coins bearing a conch on one side and a pavilion on the other were dug up at Nakhon Pathom, 'the like of which have not been found anywhere else in our part of the world except at Pagan'. In Damrong's own words, 'there are still (at Nakhon Pathom) traces of an abundance of ancient stupas and temples which date back to a period before that of King Anuruddha of Pagan'.[8] Diskul sums up the arguments in favour of the Nakhon Pathom as the centre of Suvarnabhumi. The majority of scholars however, states that the site of Nakhon Pathom ought to be the capital of this ancient kingdom and the town was probably called Suvarnabhumi at that time.

Buddhism during Mon Dvaravati Period

Around the seventh century the first independent kingdom extended over most of present-day Thailand apart from the southern area of Malaya Peninsula under the domination of the Hinduized Mon speaking people of Dvaravati. During that time, the Thais, as a race, had emigrated gradually from a home in Southern China into the Indo-Chinese peninsula.[9] Reat opines that the early Mon Buddhism of Dvaravati may have been a purer form of Theravada than that practised by the Mons of Burma. Mon architecture in Thailand seems to have received Sri Lankan influences, while Mon architecture in Burma appears to have been under north Indian Mahayana influences. Reat speculates that Thailand is the geographical centre from where Theravada Buddhism spread throughout South-East Asia. It was the Mon, not the Burmese or the Thais, who were responsible for the introduction and spread of Theravada Buddhism in the region.[10]

The Kings of Dvaravati were devout Buddhists. A number of *dharmacakras* made in this period reveal the fact that the rulers must have taken great interest in the development of Buddhism.[11] Prince Pawares, the Supreme Patriarch, writes: 'Many old stone wheels made for worshipping. May be the possessor of the wheels thought that his possession of worldly goods was not quite enough without the Jewel Wheel. He therefore made the stone wheels to worship the Three Gems of Buddhism and to gain religious merits.'[12] The people of Dvaravati not only produced *dharmacakras* but also constructed a large number of *stupas*, *mahastupas*, Buddha images, and many religious objects. Archaeologists have discovered a variety of votive *stupas*, terracotta tablets, votive tablets, terracotta begging bowls inscribed (in Pali) with the Buddhist creed (*Ye Dhamma*). The stone *dharmacakra* was inscribed with the *Pratityasamutpadasutra* (in Pali), the essence of the Buddha's teaching and considered as of paramount importance for Buddhists during sixth and seventh centuries.[13] Thus it seems that Buddhism had taken concrete shape in the time of Dvaravati Kingdom.

Buddhism during Sukhothai Period

The weakening of the Khmer empire after the death of Jayavarman VII in about AD 1218 gave the Thais opportunities to assert themselves against the Khmer's rule. As a result, the kingdom of Sukhothai came into existence, founded by King Sri Indraditya in around AD 1220. It seems that he was a staunch follower of Buddhism. He invited the monks from Sri Lanka, a great centre of Buddhism, to purify the Khmer-influenced Buddhism practised in Sukhothai.

King Rama Khamhaeng founded the Mahadhatu at Sukhodaya, the magical and spiritual centre of the kingdom. The most powerful king of Sukhothai was Rama Khamhaeng the Great, who acceded in AD 1279.[14] During his reign, Buddhism prospered. The king not only established Theravada Buddhism as the state religion, he also initiated what was to remain a notable feature of Thai Buddhism: its subservience to the throne. At Wat Sapan Hin, he built a monastery for Sangharaja, the partriarch of the Sukhodayan monkhood (Inscription I, III/28f.). From the inscriptions, we see that the king and his subjects observed the precepts during the rainy season retreat. After that came the Kathin ceremony, which lasted a month, to be followed perhaps by a gay festival. On *uposatha* days, the king invited the monks to the palace to sit on the Manasilaparta throne to expound the Dharma. On new moon days and full-moon days, he rode a richly caparisoned white elephant up to the Arannika monastery to pay his respects to the patriarch.[15]

Rama Khamhaeng set up a branching administrative hierarchy in the Sangha exactly analogous to the hierarchy of civil administrators who governed the principalities, provinces, and villages of the kingdom. Both of these hierarchies culminated in the office of the king, who was both head of government and supreme patron of the Sangha. In the city there were bronze Buddha statues of different sizes, various large and middle-sized *viharas*, and different levels of monks who resided there. An inscription of 1292 mentions that to the south of the city of Sukhothai, formidable spirit,[16] Phra-Khaphung, 'superior to all the spirit of the country', resided. 'If the prince who is sovereign in Muang Sukhothai worships this spirit properly and presents it ritual offerings, then this country will be stable and prosperous; but if does not perform the prescribed worship and does not present ritual offerings, then the spirit of this hill will no longer protect or respect the country, which will fall into decline.' Rama Khamhaeng's successors, Loe Thai and his son Lu Thai, also followed the path of religious purity rather than military conquest. Thus during the Sukhothai period great reforms were accomplished and traditional religious practices too were continued.

Dvaravati Shri Ayutthiya Period

After King Rama Khamhaeng, Sukhothai began to decline in power. By AD 1350, Ayutthiya emerged under King Ramadhipati as a centre of Thai strength. The full name of the new Thai capital was Dvaravati Shri Ayutthiya. The kings continued religious practices — Theravada Buddhism as pronounced by the Sukhothais. However, they borrowed from Khmer its political and religious organizations, material civilization, system of writing, and a considerable number of words, According to the Khmer model of kingship, which was based on a Mahayana-Hindu syncretism, the king was in some sense divine. Throughout the Ayutthiya period, Thais remained staunchly Theravada, Singhalese Buddhists[17] but the king—cast as a Bodhisattva incarnate or alternately as a *cakravartin* or 'wheel turning monarch'—assumed an even greater ascendance over the Sangha. A number of votive tablets were moulded during this period in order to transmit the merits of the Buddha. They depict many seated Buddhas, generally 500 in number, on the same plaque. As for the Bodhisattvas, only Maitreya was depicted during this period. It appears that the mass population worshipped Maitreya Buddha. In AD 1425, a delegation of Thai monks visited Sri Lanka and returned with a direct Sri Lankan ordination lineage known as *vanaratna* or 'forest jewel'. All of these orders traced back ultimately to the Mahavihara lineage of Shri Lanka and now named as *Mahanikaya* lineage, which constitutes the large majority of Thai Buddhist monks.

The Bangkok Period

In 1782, Rama I ascended the throne and founded the present Chakri dynasty. In the beginning he faced internal disorder and waged war against the Burmese. In spite of that, he built a number of royal temples, which are among the most important in the kingdom. A number of Buddha images, which suffered from Burmese wars, were collected by him. There were over twelve hundred life-size bronze Buddha images. He restored all the images and set them up in newly-built monasteries.[18] Besides, he assembled manuscripts of the canonical texts, and invited a council of monks to collate them and make an authoritative recession. The Thai scholars believe that the king followed the example of Asoka by undertaking measures towards the purification of Sangha. He enacted regulations to curb laxity among monks. During Rama II's reign (AD 1809–1924), spiritual links with Sri Lanka were re-established. Next king, Rama III (1824–51) was a very ardent supporter of Buddhism. Throughout his reign, the later King Rama IV remained a monk, learning the Pali Canon. He made various reforms in the Buddhist practices giving rise to a new sect called Dharmmayutika. Besides, he gave patronage to the old Thai Buddhist order (*Mahanikaya*) and founded a new Buddhist sect. He established diplomatic relations with various countries. Rama IV revived religious contacts with India, which had been interrupted for more than five hundred years. The Buddha images and the seeds of the Bodhi tree of the Mahabodhi temple of Bodh Gaya were sent to Thailand.

During the reign period of Rama V (1868–1910), also called King Chulalongkorn, the Buddhist links between India and Thailand became stronger. In the fourth year of his reign (1871), he visited Rammannadesa, Burma, and India. During his visit to India, he paid a visit to the Bodh Gaya temple and to Sarnath. In 1888, he invited the dignitaries of the Buddhist order to meet in council and to revise the texts of the Pali canon. When the work was complete, a thousand sets were printed, each consisting of thirty-nine volumes. For the first time, the scripture was printed in bulk in Thailand. King Chulalongkorn was succeeded by his son Prince Vajiravudh (1891), assuming the title of King Rama VI. Rama VI mobilized the Thai people to stand united for the nation, religion and throne. Rama VII, in the year 1927, brought out a new edition of the *Tripitaka* in 45 volumes, called the Siam Rath edition. Though a patron of all religions, he declared in the Thai constitution that the king is constitutionally required to profess the Buddhist faith. Anand Mahidol or Rama VIII altered the administrative system for the community of monks to correspond with the democratic system of the government. The present King Rama IX ascended the throne in 1946. He also did developmental work for the Buddhist order and had entered the monkhood for a short period.

RELIGIOUS SYNCRETISM IN THAI BUDDHISM

Thais profess Theravada Buddhism as their state religion. Theravada's doctrinal tradition derives from the distinctive *Abhidhamma Pitaka*. Some scholars have suggested that this Theravada is better identified as the *Vibhajjavada School*. Theravada Buddhism shows man the way to salvation through his own endeavour. In other words, Theravada belongs to 'the Holy Path', the doctrine of salvation by self-effort.[19] The Thai Theravada doctrinal tradition is also characterized by an ordination tradition based on its distinctive *Vinaya Pitaka*. Although various branches of Theravada may historically have used other Vinaya which have modern interpretation of the traditional 227 rules of conduct of the monks.

Francois Bizot has pointed out the eclectic nature of Buddhism in pre-modern Thailand. It has congruence of Vedic Brahmanism, tantrism, and pre-Aryan Austro-Asiatic cults of guardian spirits and protective divinities. Interacting with Mon Theravada beliefs and practices, and possibly influenced by the Mulasarvastivadins, it resulted in what Bizot has characterized as 'tantric Theravada' identified with a mystical tradition known as *yogacara* (practitioner of spiritual discipline).[20] The features of this tantric Theravada, at odds with the stereotypical view of classical Theravada, include identifying one's body with the qualities of the Buddha; the use of esoteric syllables and words (*dharani*, *mantra*, *yantra*) to represent the identity of microcosm and macrocosm; the potency of sounds and letters; and esoteric initiation for the realization of both spiritual and mundane ends.[21]

According to Buddhadasa Bhikkhu, rites and ceremonies are numerous in Thai Buddhism. Take for example the procedure for the ordainment of a monk. It has become customary to give gifts to the newly-ordained monk. Guests are invited to bring food and to watch the proceedings. Ceremonies are performed both at the temple and in the home.[22] Besides, as Sweares records, tantric rituals have been practised by the Thais. Temple festivals begin by invoking the guardian deities of the four quarters. An elaborate spirit-calling ceremony (*riak khwan*) often precedes monastic ordination. Yantric tattoos and magical amulets are worn by the devout to ward off danger. Offerings are made at the shrines of deities protecting mountain passes and at elaborate altars of the Hindu god Brahma.[23] In Chiangmai, northern Thais inaugurate the New Year by three sequential event: appealing to the spirit of a Buddha image; invoking the god, Indra, resident in the city pillar; and sacrificing a buffalo to the spirits who guard the mountains which overlook the valley (which supports the theory of tantric Theravada propounded by Bizot).[24] The veneration of King Rama V (Chulalongkorn, r. 1868–1910), which originated as a cult of his equestrian statue before the parliament building in Bangkok, has now spread nationwide, revealing a syncretism in Thai Buddhism, with the ancestral cult.

BRAHMANICAL ELEMENTS IN THAI BUDDHISM

The magical and protecting power were included in the images of Buddha during the reign of Rama Khamhaeng. Thai chronicles reveal that certain images of the Buddha which were regarded as the protectors of principalities, acted as magical protectors and bringers of security and prosperity.[25] Brahmans had acquired an important place in Thai common society as well as in the royal court. Priestly functions at the time of coronation were performed only by the Brahmans.[26] H.G. Quaritch Wales noticed several Brahmanical rituals being performed at the royal court. According to him, Rama Khamhaeng must have had a body of Brahmans attached to his court to advise on matters of statecraft, law, and technical matters concerning the calendar and horoscopes; to manage the Swinging Festival, the First Ploughing, and rites for the control of wind and rain; to prepare the water for the vassals to drink as a token of allegiance; to look after the regalia and arrange the Royal Progresses; to perform the ceremonies of tonsure, investiture and cremation for royalty; and to discharge a number of other tasks. He has documented all these ceremonies.[27]

Tonsure Ceremony

The Tonsure ceremony is a rite of youths corresponding to the Hindu Culakanath Mangala. It is most important Brahmanical ceremony, which is still surviving at the royal court. Tonsure takes place at the age of either eleven or thirteen. The logic behind conducting tonsure at this age is that the boy enters to novitiate before he is fourteen years of age. The difference between Buddhist and Brahmanical tonsure is that the Buddhists shave the whole head of a person without performing any ritual. In the case of Thais, it is performed ritually. This ceremony is prevalent not only in the royal court but it is also very common among the general people of Thailand. The tonsure of the prince is called *sokanta*, while the performance among the common people is called *kara kon cuk*. The generic and at the same time classic Pali term used in Thailand is *culakantahmangala* (corresponding to the Sanskrit *kesanta*). The *sokanta* differs in the main from the *kara kon cuk* by reason of the fact that in the former a special artificial mountain (Kailasa) within the palace grounds is used, whereas in the latter the ceremonies are carried out on an ordinary ceremonial dais under a canopy, erected in the private house of the initiate's family. For princes of *Brah Anga Cau* and *Hmom Cau* rank, a permanent rocky structure about 10 ft high, and situated within the precinct of the palace, is utilized as a Kailasa; but for *Cau Fa* a special mountain is built, 20 to 46 ft in height. The reason for the use of a structure symbolizing Kailasa is that, following Brahmanical tradition, the *sokanta* is carried out in accordance with the ceremonial that accompanied the mythical tonsure of Siva's son Ganesha on Mount Kailasa. A rites hall called *Tusita Maha Prasada* is prepared, where the Buddhist monks recite *paritta* texts at most state ceremonies. The most important part of the ceremony comes when the prince reaches the top of Kailasa, where the king himself receives the candidate. The whole ritual is based on the Brahmanical tonsure ceremony, but due to the introduction of Buddhism in the country great changes took place, even as the core concept of Brahmanical ritual survives.

RITUAL FOR THE ANCESTORS (*PITRA SRADDHA*)

The rituals connected with the ancestors are prevalent across Thai society. These Thai rituals are supposed to be an inextricable mixture of Indian and Mongolian forms.[28] In India, the offering of food to the ancestors is called *pitra sraddha*. The Thais use the same tradition. In the first place, it is customary for every one who can afford it to give a feast at New Year at which the spirits of the dead are supposed to attend. Lighted candles and flowers are placed before an urn and Buddhist monks come to take part in the feast and recite appropriate *sutras* from the Buddhist texts. The worship of the dead kings is also popular in Thailand. As far as Thailand is concerned, the proximate origin of the worship of the dead kings is to be found in the cult of the Devaraja in Cambodia, which was also known in Java and south India. This practice was retained by the rulers of the Sukhodaya period. Right to the present day, two methods of showing honour to the deceased kings of the dynasty remain, one of which is apparently Hindu, the other Buddhist.

Ceremonies Related to Agriculture

Thais still perform a number of ceremonies relating to agriculture. They are the *baruna satra* (rain or Varuna festival) which relates to rain; the *lai roa* or *lain am*, the speeding of the outflow, which pertains to dispersion of floodwater; *Dhanya-daha* (harvest thanksgiving).

Minor Brahmanical Festivals

Some minor Brahmanical festivals were performed in the royal court. The worship of the sacred bull (*Chavian Brah Go Kin*) was performed in the second month called as *Pausa*. This ritual has been discontinued for the last several centuries. The Visnu slumber ceremony was also performed but now it has also been completely disappeared. *Sivaratri* or Siva Night was performed in very early times. The *Snana* or *Gajendrasva-snanam* ceremony signifies the sprinkling of the elephants and horses was carried out in the fifth (*Chaitra*) and eleventh (*Asvina*) months. The New Year celebration is also performed. There are really three Siamese New Year Festivals, which used to take up most of the fifth month (*Chaitra*) but now officially combined to be celebrated on the first April. This date is actually New Year's Day of the civil calendar introduced in 1889.

Syncretism in Thai Buddhism is reflected from the social life of the Brahman community who claim origins in Ramnagram. The latter can be identified either with the modern Ramnagar a part of the modern Varanasi or with the Ramesvaram, a tiny coastal town in southern India. The social life of the Brahmans is quite unusual. Their families have only one or two members practice as Brahmans in their daily routine. Other members, including the wife of the priest, continue to adhere to Buddhism. They take part unequivocally in Buddhism-based activities such as making offering to monks and visiting Buddhist shrines.

SYNCRETISM IN THE ART OF THAILAND

A series of splendid bronze statues of Hindu gods of the Sukhothai period are tangible proof that Brahmanism was active, and Brahmanical elements are seen in the Buddhist art of Thailand.

Until very recent days, Brahmans played a significant role in the making of Buddha image. While casting the image of Buddha, the Brahman would initiate it in order to transfer more power to the images. The Hindu deities (such as Phra Phrom=Brahma, Phra Narai=Visnu, Phra Isuan=Siva) live in the heart and minds of the common and the elite population of Thailand. These deities are shown in Thai art in such a way that they appear to be a part of Buddhism. In some of the Buddhist monasteries, the images of Brahma, Visnu, and Siva are worshipped. Brahma is more popular than the other deities. Ganesha images also appear frequently in Thai art. A large number of the images of Avalokitesvara Bodhisattva and Maitreya, made in different periods, reveal the syncretism of Mahayana Buddhism with Theravada Buddhism in the art of Thailand. Some of the characteristics of the Buddha images show a fusion with Brahmanical elements. For example, the Sukhothai Buddha images are characterized by a tall flame-like structure[29] in place of *usnisa*. It seems quite possible that the prominent role played by the Brahmans in artistic expression introduced such features during the Sukhothai period.

As far as architecture is concerned, a deep study shows the absorption of other religious elements. The Khmer temples (*prangs*) in Thailand show Brahmanical cosmological elements. Each *prang* looks like a mountain, the abode of the gods in both Hindu and Buddhist cosmology.

The Thai *mondop* resembles closely the *mandapa* of Indian temples. Square in plan and cubical in form, it has a pyramidal superstructure for roofing. The Thai *mondop* enshrines a holy object like a foot-print of the Buddha, or else may serve as a kind of library and storeroom for objects used in religious ceremonies as is the case with the *mondop* of Wat Kaew in Krung Thep (Bangkok).

Since the foundation of the first independent Thai kingdom, Sukhothai in the thirteenth century, the teachings of the Buddha have percolated to every hamlet and hut in every corner of Thailand. Theravada Buddhism of Thailand has imbibed characteristic features of both the Sri Lankan tradition as well as Cambodian Buddhism. The people of Dvaravati laid the foundation of Thai Buddhism, and the tradition continues till date. Theravada Buddhism has never been isolated from the state and, in fact, has always been patronized by the state.

With the process of modernization, the role of Buddhist monks and monasteries may have receded to the religious and spiritual spheres of life. There was an intimate relationship between Buddhist monks and the Buddhist laity. They have played a significant role in social change. Theravada has coexisted in Thailand with the ancestral cult and with Brahmanical rituals.

Acknowledgements: The author is indebted to Dr. K.K. Chakravarti, Member Secretary, IGNCA, and to Prof. G.C. Tripathi, Head of Kala Kosa, and to Shri A.N. Jha, for their administrative and academic support.

NOTES

1. *The Encyclopedia of Religion*, vol. 6, p. 260.
2. C. Tongprasert, *History of Buddhism in South East Asia*, p. 285; Sir Charles Eliot, *Hinduism and Buddhism*, vol. III, p. 98.
3. Sir Charles Eliot, *Hinduism and Buddhism*, vol. III, p. 98.
4. R.C. Majumdar, *Suvarnadvipa*, vol. II, part 1, p. 48.
5. George Coedès, *Indianized States of Southeast Asia*, Honolulu, p. 40.
6. *Sasanavamsa*, p. 10 (composed by Pannasami, a Burmese monk in 1841) cf. Brian Harrison, *South East Asia: A Short History*, p. 10; Sir Charles Eliot, *Hinduism and Buddhism*, vol. III, pp. 50–1.
7. M.C. Subhadradis Diskul, 'Phra Pathom Chedi' (in) *Excursion to Nakhon Pathom*, Siam Society, Bangkok, 2000.
8. U Than Hla, 'Thaton and Nakhon Pathom', *Shiroku*, no. 16, December 1983, pp. 1–10.
9. Phya Anuman Rajadhon, *The Cultures of Thailand*, Bangkok, 1953, p. 4.
10. Noble Ross Reat, *Buddhism: A History*, California, 1951, p. 121.
11. Dhanit Yupho, *Dharmacakra or the Wheel of the Law*, Thai Culture New Series no. 25, Bankok, BE 2517.
12. Ibid., p. 11.
13. Phasook Indrawooth, *Dvaravati: A Critical Study Based on Archaeological Evidence*, BE 2042, p. 235.
14. A.B. Griswold, *Towards a History of Sukhodaya Art*, Bangkok, 1967, p. 6.
15. Ibid, p. 10.
16. G. Coedès, *Les Puples de la peninsula Indochinoise*, Paris, 1962, p. 136.
17. G. Coedès, op. citi., p. 223.
18. A.B. Griswold, 'Medieval Siamese Images in the Bo Tree Monastery', *Artibus Asiae*, XVIII/1.
19. Yoneo Ishii, *Sangha, State, and Society: Thai Buddhism in History*, Honolulu, University of Hawaii Press, 1986, p. 3.
20. Donald K. Swears, *Encyclopaedia of Buddhism*, vol. II, Robert E. Buswell (Jr. Editor in chief), Macmillan Reference, USA, 2004, pp. 830–1.
21. Ibid, p. 830.
22. Bhikkhu Buddhadasa, *Hand Book for Mankind*, Mahachula Buddhist University Press, Bangkok, Thailand (first published in 1956), p. 16.
23. Donald K. Sweares, op. cit., p. 830.
24. Francois Bizot, *Le Chemin de Lanka*, Paris: Ecole Francaise d'Extreme Orient, 1992.
25. A.B. Griswold, op. cit., p. 7.
26. H.G. Quaritch Wales, *Ancient Siamese Government and Administration*, New York, 1965, p. 240.

27. H.G. Quaritch Wales, *Siamese State Ceremonies: Their History and Function*, London, 1931, chapters V-XXIV.
28. Ibid., p. 169.
29. M.C. Subhadradis Diskul, *Art of Thailand: A Brief History*, Bangkok, 1991 7th edn., p. 19.

World Heritage Sites in Thailand Reflecting Indo-Thai Cultural Linkage

AMARA SRISUCHAT

INTRODUCTION

In Thailand were laid the foundations of a civilization that began in prehistoric times and flourished through the ages. Evidence of civilization in the land can be found in the form of monumental sites. Various ancient monuments and numerous art objects combine with traditions and religious beliefs to form the cultural heritage. It is indisputable that the cultural heritage reflecting the religious beliefs present the main context of Thai-India relationships in the past.

Among a large number of national heritage sites, three, Ban Chiang Archaeological Site, Sukhothai and associated cities, and Ayutthiya became World Heritage Sites in 1991. Two of these, the Sukhothai cluster and Ayutthiya are the point of discussion in this paper.

SUKHOTHAI

The ancient Town of Sukhothai (Fig. 1) is situated in Muang Sukhothai district, Sukhothai Province, 12 km west of Sukhothai provincial administrative town. Sukhothai is situated in the lower part of the northern region, 435 km from Bangkok, the capital of Thailand.

The ancient town is rectangular, 1,400 × 1,810 m (Fig. 2), surrounded by three rings of earth ramparts. Between each rampart exists a moat about 20 m.

Inside the town stand numerous ruins which can be divided into sixteen Buddhist temples and two Hindu shrines. There are two Hindu shrines outside the city wall to the north and to the west, Wat Phra Phai Luang (Fig. 3) and Ho Thewalai Maha Kaset, respectively.

The Buddhist temples inside the town, and about 200 Buddhist temples outside the town in an area of 70 sq km, were built in the

Fig. 1: The Ancient Town of Sukhothai.

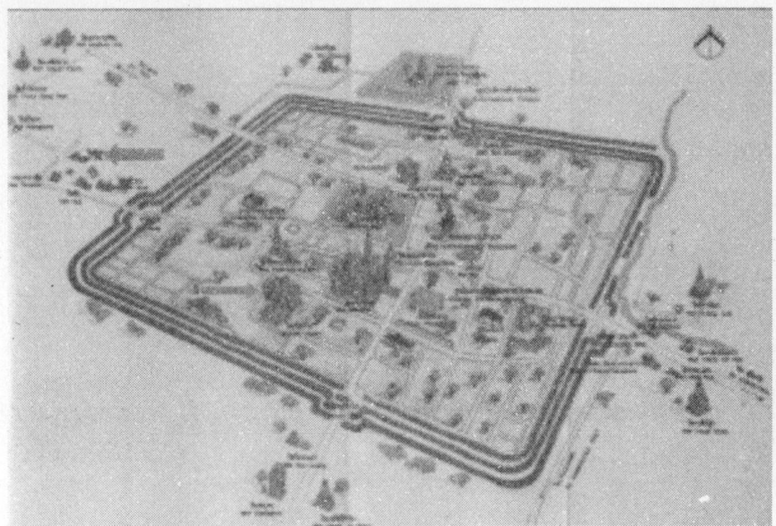

Fig. 2: Plan of the Ancient Town of Sukhothai and its monuments.

Fig. 3: Wat Phra Phai Luang twelfth-thirteenth century

Fig. 4: Ta Pha Daeng Shrine, twelfth century.

thirteenth to fifteenth centuries. Three Hindu shrines, Ta Pha Daeng (Fig. 4), Wat Si Sawai (Fig. 5), Wat Phra Phai Luang were built in the eleventh to thirteenth centuries. Only Ho Thewalai Maha Kaset (Fig. 6) was built in the fourteenth century, the other three Hindu shrines being remains of the Khmer style.

It is indisputable that the ancient Cambodia, the land of the Khmer, developed a strongly Hindunized culture. During the period of Khmer predominance the religion spread across present-day Thailand. From this Sukhothai inherited the cult of Hindu deities, especially the chief gods—Brahmā the Creator, Śiva the Destroyer, and Viṣṇu the Protector—who were adopted by the Thais.

Hindu religious beliefs from India came to the Thais in Sukhothai through Khmer art. This is exemplified by a lintel found at Wat Si Sawai (Fig. 7). The lintel depicts Anantaśayana of Viṣṇu or the reclining of Viṣṇu who is here depicted on the coils of the celebrated serpent Śeṣa that shields the head of god under its seven hoods. Near the feet of Viṣṇu is represented a seated Lakṣmī, who holds the feet of the god. And from his navel springs a lotus stalk with a full blossomed lotus flower on which Brahmā is comfortably seated

Fig. 5: Wat Si Sawai, eleventh-thirteenth century.

Fig. 6: Ho Thewalai Maha Kaset, fourteenth century.

Fig. 7: Lintel found at Wat Si Sawai depicting reclining Viṣṇu.

in the worshipping attitude. Śiva is probably represented in the form of a seated Yogi in a worshipping attitude. This lintel, dated to approximately 1100, is considered the earliest find reflecting an adoption of Hinduism in Sukhothai.

Certain characteristics of four stone images of the twelfth century from the Ta Pha Daeng shrine (Fig. 8) suggest links with, or borrowings from, the Khmer. The images are headless figures. The tallest is probably a representation of a deity or a devata, and the female is his consort. Two smaller figures may be identified as dvārapāla or guardian figures of the shrine.

In the thirteenth–fourteenth century the art evolved according to Thai aesthetics and ideals, with the result that the bronze statues and statuettes of deities produced in Sukhothai are masterpieces in Thai own right. Their style is no longer Indian, nor any longer Khmer: it is instead an outstanding expression of the vibrant local, Sukhothai art.

Sukhothai kings assumed the role of supreme guardian of all religious foundations in their realm. To enhance their royal status they patronized Dharma, and for this they sought guidance and encouragement from the Brahmans, especially in the management of state rituals. The Brahmans performed ceremonies for the worship of Īśvara, Maheśvara, Viṣṇu, Brahmā, Hari-Hara, Kṛṣṇa, Rāma, Indra, and Agni. Bronze images of deities at Sukhothai are crowned

Deity

Devi

Ta Pha Daeng Shrine

Dvārpāla (guardian)

Dvārpāla (guardian)

Fig. 8: Four stone images found at Ta Pha Daeng Shrine, twelfth century.

and wear royal attire, being cult objects in royal court rituals performed by the Brahmans (Fig. 9). It is evident that some of these statues were originally placed at Ho Thewalai Maha Kast (the Devālaya Mahākṣetra shrine) which was established by King Lithai of Sukhothai in 1349. A number of stucco sculptures too were found, at Wat Chedi Si Hong outside the ancient town to the south, represent the heads of Brahmans in different ways (Fig. 10).

The integration of Hinduism with Buddhism is exemplified by a stucco sculpture depicting the Buddha seated on the hair bun of a Brahman, found in a temple in the Ancient Town of Sukhothai (Fig. 11).

Regarding architectural features, the oldest monuments in the Wat Phra Phai Luang temple are three buildings constructed in 'prang' forms which imitate Hindu śikhara vimānas. At present, two of them are still in existence but only their bases remain. A third in the north

Viṣṇu Hari-Hara Umā

Fig. 9: Bronze images found at Sukhothai, some at the Devālaya Mahākṣetra shrine, fourteenth century.

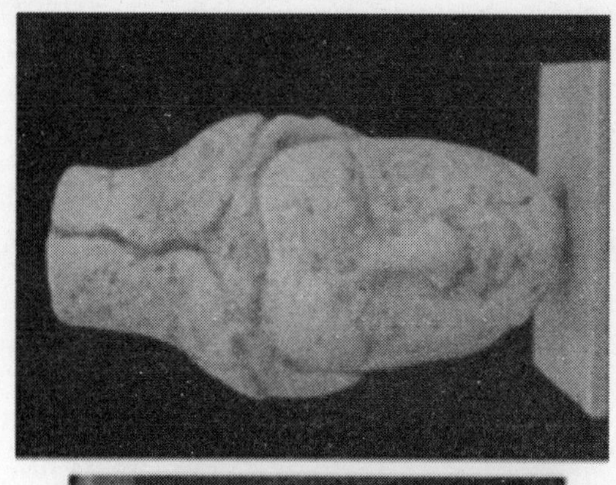

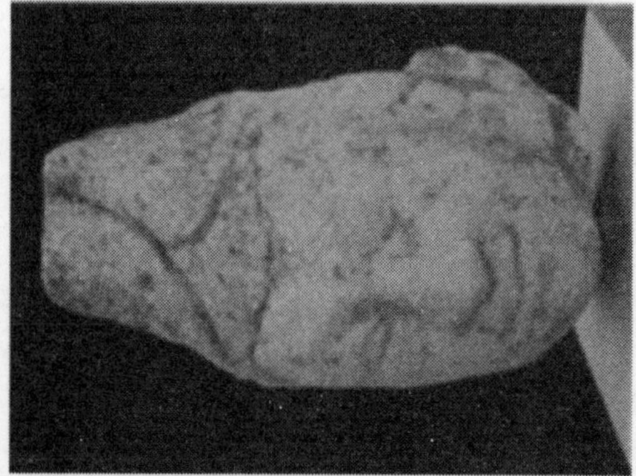

Fig. 10: Stucco heads from Wat Chedi Si Hong.

Fig. 11: Buddha seated on the bun of a Yogi, stucco, from a temple site in the Ancient Town of Sukhothai.

is adorned with stuccoed relief depicting the story of Buddha. In addition, there are stuccoed reliefs depicting Hindu deities, such as Śiva and Brahmā. These stuccoed reliefs help to confirm the supposition that a mix of Hindu and Buddhist cults occurred in the kingdom of Sukhothai.

Wat Si Sawai is another temple that has 'prangs' imitating Hindu temple towers. Found *in situ*, a lintel depicting reclining Viṣṇu and fragments of Hindu god images, e.g. bronze statuettes of Hari-Hara and of Śiva (Fig. 9), Śivaliṅga, and two stucco sculptures which are identified with head of Brahmā and head of Śiva, respectively, indicate that this sanctuary was originally a Hindu shrine, later transformed into a Buddhist temple.

There are a large number of Buddhist temples inside and outside the Ancient Town of Sukhothai. Among these Wat Si Chum is a representative example of a Theravada temple showing a significant conception of Buddhist art and literature. This temple comprises a huge square maṇḍapa, a main vihāra in front of the maṇḍapa, and a small stupa and small vihāra to the left of the maṇḍapa. The brick maṇḍapa was built to enshrine a seated Buddha image of large size. The image is in Māravijaya posture, the attitude of subduing Māra. It is called 'Phra Acana' in the Sukhothai inscription No. 1, 1292: '. . . North of this city of Sukhothai there is the bazaar, there is the Phra Acana statue, there are the Prāsādas,. . .' (Na Nagara and Griswold 1992: 275)

The maṇḍapa wall to the right of the Buddha image is doubled and a narrow dark tunnel-like stairway corridor has been traced. The ceiling of the corridor is covered with slate slabs engraved with scenes depicting Jātaka stories, with a short inscription in Thai describing each scene. It is conjectured that there were originally 88 Jātaka engravings installed in the corridor. Fifty-one of these are visible, the rest have deteriorated.

SI SATCHANALAI

The ancient town of Si Satchanalai is situated on the western bank of the Yom River, near Luang Rapids. It is about 55 km from Sukhothai to the north. The Si Satchanalai town is rectangular, 900 × 700 m, and protected by a laterite wall enclosing two small hills within the town. Inside the town remain 25 ruins, and outside, about 190 ruins.

Three kilometres south-west of Si Satchanalai lies another old town, Chalieng. Architectural and archaeological remains found in this historic town indicate that it was not politically important, but was an important religious centre.

The important temples in Chalieng have buildings with 'prang' (Fig. 12) or 'prāsādas'. These temples are Wat Phra Si Ratanamahathat and Wat Chao Chan.

The main 'prang' of Wat Phra Si Ratanamahathat was first constructed in the early thirteenth century. It is believed that the original Khmer 'prang' is probably inside this large one which was constructed during the early Ayutthiya period about 1450 and restored again in the late period of Ayutthiya, about 1700. Decorative

Fig. 12: Two 'prangs' in imitation Śikhara Vimānas, Si Satchanalai, thirteenth-fourteenth century.

stucco of the Bayon art style of ancient Khmer was found at the main entrance of the temple. The top part is decorated with stucco motifs representing a human face on each of the four cardinal points, in imitation of the Khmer Bayon style (*c.* 1177–1230). It is conjectured that this is the four-faced Lokeśvara in Mahāyāna Buddhism (Fig. 13). This figure is comparable to four-faced Brahmā made of stucco and ceramic found at Wat Phra Phai Luang, the Ancient Town of Sukhothai.

Underneath the four-faced Lokeśvara figure sit deities under niches and then a dancing female figure reminiscent of Khmer art. On the left is the head of Kāla with arms. It is indisputable that the placement of Kāla in front of the entrance to the temple has been practised in India and the Khmer adopted this tradition. The presence of Kāla at the entrance of the temple probably again derived from Khmer origins (Fig. 14).

The most attractive structure at Wat Chao Chan is the main 'prang' built of laterite blocks. It is believed that originally the main structure had been a Khmer prang constructed at the command of King Jayavarman VII of Cambodia (*c.* 1181–1220) along a highway. It is

Fig. 13: The top of the entrance to the prang of Wat Phra Si Ratana Mahathat is decorated with stucco motifs of Kāla (below, left) and four-faced Lokeśvara (above) who is worshipped in Mahayana Buddhism.

the northernmost Khmer 'prang' ever found in Thailand (Diskul 1999: 192). The building was built in accordance with the Mahayanist concept of a tower to house a Bodhisattva. It was changed into a

Fig. 14: Kāla, stucco, from a temple of the Ancient Town of Si Satchanalai, *c*. 1400. Kāla appears at the entrance of both Hindu and Buddhist sanctuaries, as a protector.

Theravada temple in the Sukhothai period, after 1200, and a laterite vihāra and a maṇḍapa for housing the image of the Buddha were added in the front and north of the prang, respectively.

KAMPHAENG PHET

Kamphaeng Phet (Fig. 15) is about 82 km from Sukhothai, on the eastern bank of the Ping river and in Muang Kamphaeng Phet District, Kamphaeng Phet Province. It has 14 monuments inside the town wall, 0.80 sq km surrounded by laterite ramparts and ditches, and 40 monuments outside the town wall to the north, with 15 monuments outside the town wall to the east.

Among the monuments inside the town wall, two, Wat Phra Kaeo and San Phra Isuan (Īśvara shrine), are the place where objects of Indian impact or origin were recovered.

Wat Phra Kaeo is in the heart of the town (Fig. 16). This large temple was laid on a rectangular plan. Important buildings consist

Fig. 15: The ancient town of Kamphaeng Phet.

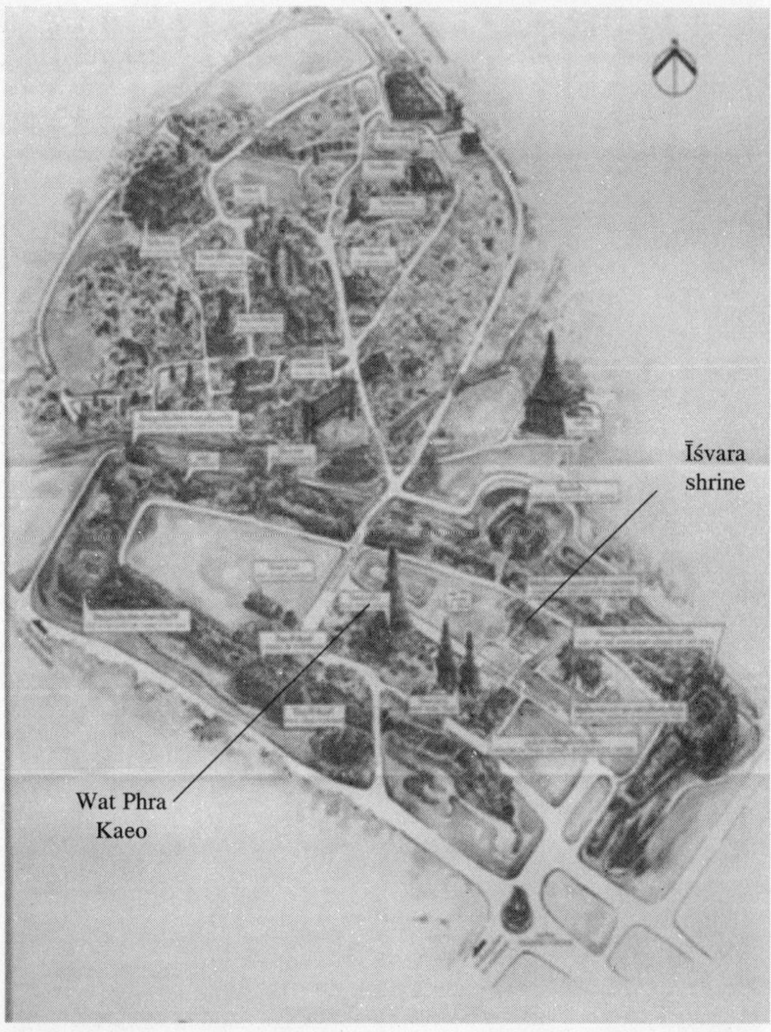

Fig. 16: Plan of the Ancient Town of Kamphaeng Phet depicting monuments inside and outside the town wall and two sites, Wat Phra Kaeo and San Phra Isuan.

of a bell-shaped chedi, a large base of the main vihāra, and a small vihāra housing three large Buddha images. This small vihāra has two images, the subduing of Māra, and a reclining image. The physical features of the images are different from those of Buddha images in the Sukhothai style, suggesting that these three Buddha images belong to the U-thong style of the early Ayutthiya period, around 1350. The significant evidence reflecting the Indian tradition is decorative stucco found around the base of this vihāra depicts scenes from the *Rāmāyaṇa* (Figs. 17, 18). Broken pieces of these reliefs are on display at Kamphaeng Phet National Museum.

Another significant building is the San Phra Isuan, literally, the Īśvara shrine (Fig. 19). This is the only Hindu sanctuary in Kamphaeng Phet, and only the rectangular laterite base remains. The shrine housed a bronze statue of Śiva. (Bronze statues of Viṣṇu and Devi were also found.)

The image of Śiva, 2.10 m in height, displays the lingering influence of the Khmer Bayon style (Diskul 1999: 269) (Fig. 20). There is an inscription on the base informing us that Chao Phraya Si Thammasokarat had this image cast in 1510. An inscription of three lines running around the god's feet commemorates the works

Fig. 17: Vihāra of Wat Phra Kaeo. The wall of this vihāra is bears stucco reliefs depicting scenes from the *Rāmāyaṇa*, now in the Kamphaeng Phet National Museum.

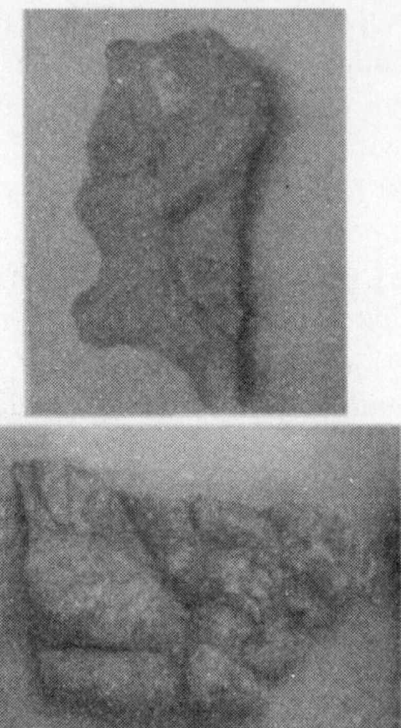

Fig. 18: Part of stucco relief depicting scene from the *Rāmāyaṇa*, Wat Phra Kaeo, fourteenth century.

Fig. 19: Base of San Phra Isuan or Īśvara shrine, Kamphaeng Phet, 1510.

Fig. 20: Bronze statue of Īśvara found at the shrine, 1510

of merit of Chao Phraya Si Thammasokarat, ruler of Kamphaeng Phet (ruling as a subject of the Ayutthiyan king, Rāmāthipbodi II (*c.* 1491 –1529). He then dedicates the merit accruing from his works to 'the two kings': presumably Rāmāthipbodi II who was reigning at Ayutthiya, and one of the latter's relatives who was reigning as viceroy at Phitsanulok.

The following translation of the inscription is derived from Epigraphic and Historical Studies written by Prasert Ṇa Nagara and A.B. Griswold, 1992, p. 635:

In Sakarāja 1432, a year of the horse, on Sunday the fourteenth day of the waxing moon of the sixth month, (when the moon had) attained the ṛkṣa of hasta, at two nālikā after dawn, Chao Phraya Si Thammasokarat founded (this statue of the) Lord Īśvara to protect the four-footed and two-footed creatures in Muang Kamphang Phet, and to help exalt the religions—the Buddha's religion, the Brahmanical religion, and the Devakarma—so that they will not lost their lustre. May they function harmoniously together!

He restored the Mahādhātu, and the lesser temples both inside and outside the city, as well as the boundaries of household properties, and the highway which had fallen into ruin all the way to Bang Phan, and he dredged the River Trai (at?) Bang Phro.

Moreover, he put a stop to the custom of selling cattle to the Lavā.

Moreover, when he plants a rice-field he always plants it with seed taken from the field itself; he does not take rice from a granary to broadcast or (to make a seedbed from which) to transplant, as most people do.

Moreover, as the irrigation canal made by his ancestor Phrya Ruang to lead water to Bang Phan had got filled up and altogether lost, so that it was commonly believed the rice-fields were dependent on rain, he searched for that canal, and when he found it he restored it so as to lead water into the fields and irrigate them instead of depending on rain.

The merit (accruing from) all these things that he has done, he presents to Their Majesties the two Kings.

AYUTTHIYA

Ayutthiya is situated in Phra Nakhon Si Ayutthiya Province, about 76 km north of Bangkok. The site of the ancient town lay at a point past which three main rivers flowed on their way from the north towards the Gulf of Thailand. The rivers are the Chao Phraya, the Pasak and the Lopburi.

According to historical evidence, Ayutthiya was the capital of Thailand between 1350 and 1767 in three periods: the early Ayutthiya period (1350–1488), the middle Ayutthiya period (1489–1655), and the late Ayutthiya period (1656–1767).

Since 1987, the monuments in the ancient town have been explored by the Fine Arts Department, under the management unit

Wat Phuttaisawan Wat Som Wat Langka

Fig. 21: Stupas in the form of 'prangs' of the early Ayutthiya period, 1350–1488.

called Ayutthiya Historical Park. The responsibility of the Historical Park covers the maintenance of 95 monuments inside and outside the Ancient Town. In the Ancient Town there is a National Museum called Chao Sam Phraya National Museum built to collect objects found from monuments and archaeological sites in the Ancient Town of Ayutthiya.

There are many types of buildings built in Ayutthiya in different periods. Among these, a number of stupas in the form of 'prang' are prominent. Significant prangs in the early Ayutthiya period are located in Wat Ratchaburana, Wat Phutthaisawan, Wat Phra Ram, Wat Mahathat, Wat Som, and Wat Langka (Fig. 21). Buildings in the form of prangs of the middle Ayutthiya period are present in Wat Worachet Thepbamrung and Wat Worachettharam. The main prang of Wat Chaiwatthanaram and a prang of Wat Boromphuttharam were built in the late Ayutthiya period (Santi Leksukhum 2001: 58–69). Among these the main prang of Wat Ratchaburana is the best known, for a large number of royal treasures were discovered inside its crypts.

Wat Ratchaburana (Fig. 22) was built in the reign of King Boramrachathirat (Chao Sam Phraya) in 1424 on the cremation site of his brothers, Prince Ai Phraya and Prince Yi Phraya who were killed in a duel on elephant. Two Chedis with ashes of the two princes were built on the combat spot. At present only their bases can be seen (Ayutthiya Historical Park 2003: 215). In the main prang of Wat Ratchaburana, two crypts were discovered. The crypts were filled with golden royal treasures and Buddha sealings. These finds are exhibited in Chao Sam Phraya National Museum. The valuable objects can be divided into two main kinds: donations and objects of Buddhist worship. These include royal utensils, Buddha images, a small stupa, a gold inscription, gold sculpture, gold architectural model and gold ornaments. Among the royal utensils, a gold gourd-shaped ceremonial water-pouring vessel is prominent. The lid of the vessel is conspicuous, for it is in the form of four-faced Brahmā. (Fig. 23)

It is believed that tradition of making four-faced Brahmā continued in Ayutthiya kingdom. This may be the influence from Sukhothai. Moreover, there is another four-faced Brahmā made of stone in large size found in Ayutthiya, unfortunately the function of it and its precise

Fig. 22: Wat Ratchaburana.

Fig. 23: The lid of the gold gourd-shaped ceremonial water-pouring vessel is in the form of four-faced Brahmā.
This object was found in the crypt of 'prang' of Wat Ratchaburana, 1424

site is unknown. At present this stone four-faced Brahmā is housed in Chao Sam Phraya National Museum.

It is indisputable that Brahmanical tradition was active at the Ayutthiyan court but the worship of Hindu god was practised as well. This is exemplified by a stone sculpture of Gaṇeśa found in Ayutthiya. This object is now also in Chao Sam Phraya National Museum.

Apart from the sculptures of Hindu god, a bronze image of a Ṛṣi, or ascetic, 64 cm in height, found in Wat Phrasisanphet, is identified with a Bodhisattva who was born as an ascetic in a previous life of Buddha. It is a good example to emphasize the integration of Brahmanism into Buddhism in the early period of Ayutthiya.

SELECT BIBLIOGRAPHY

Ayutthiya Historical Park, *Guide to Ayutthiya Historical Park*, Bangkok: Si Muang Kan Phim, 2003.

Environment Conservation on National and Cultural Heritage Division, *Thai-Heritage-World Heritage*, Bangkok: Faculty of Environment and Resource Studies, n.d.

Office of Archaeology, *Guide to Sukhothai, Si Satchanalai and Kamphaeng Phet Historical Parks*, Sukhothai: Witthaya Computor Offset, 2003.

Prasert, Na Nagara, A.B. Griswold, *Epigraphic and Historical Studies*, Bangkok: The Historical Society under the Royal Patronage of H.R.H. Princess Maha Chakri Sirindhorn, 1992.

Santi Leksukhum, *Silpa Ayutthiya*, 2nd edn., Bangkok: Samnakphim Muang Boran, 2001 (in Thai).

Srisuchat, Amara, *Major Events in History of Sukhothai*, Bangkok: Office of Environmental Policy and Planning, 2003.

Subhadradis, Diskul, *Sukhothai Art*, Bangkok: Princess Maha Chakri Sirindhorn Anthropology Centre, 1999.

The Preserved Tradition of Mahayana in Thailand

BINAY KUMAR MISHRA

Siddhartha Gautam came to be known after his enlightenment under the pious Bodhi tree at Bodh Gaya—the place to which fortunately I too belong—as 'Buddha', meaning the 'enlightened one'. In the *Dighanikaya*, is a description of the Buddha:

iti pi so bhagava araham sammasambuddho vijjacaranasampanno
sugato lokavidu anuttaro purisadamma-sarathi sattha devamanussanam

The statement refers to nine characteristics (*navaguna*) of Buddha. These characteristics are best understood in the context of the body of doctrine available to us. The influence of Buddha's teachings on mankind remained pervasive and spread rapidly both in India and beyond her boundaries to gain a lasting hold in the lives of countless millions throughout the centuries in South, East and South-East Asia.

It is quite probable that Buddhism remained basically a sectarian religion until the time of Asoka, but with his reign entered a new phase in which it became a civilizational religion. Of the different factors transforming Buddhism into a civilizational religion the foremost was its doctrinal and scholastic modality. During the Asokan and post-Asokan periods, factions within the monastic community began to formulate the aspects of the teachings more precisely, and to develop these teachings into philosophies that attempted to explain all of reality in a coherent and logically defensible manner. As a result, the literature in which the community preserved its memory of the sermons of the Buddha (the *sutras*) and his instructions to the monastic order (the *vinaya*) came to be supplemented by new scholastic texts—the *Abhidhamma*. Given the philosophical ambiguities of received traditions, it was inevitable that contradictory doctrines would be put forward, and that different religio-philosophical systems would be generated. This led to controversies within the community and these controversies to the proliferation of Buddhist schools and subschools, probably in conjunction with other more mundane disputes. A total of eighteen schools (without any consistency in names) have been listed. The institutional and ideological boundaries between groups were fluid.

Soon after Buddha's *mahaparinirvana* in 487 BC the First Buddhist Council was held at Rajagriha and presided over by Mahakassap. Comprising about 500 Arhats, this council was responsible for the composition of the monastic discipline (*vinaya*) under the monk Upali and the Dhamma under the monk Anand. The proceedings of the Council were approved by all the monks present, except by Purana Dakkhinagiri, who wanted the incorporation of slight changes in the rules relating to the cooking, storage, and eating of food by monks. A little over a century later actual dissension took place in the Sangha. In the Second Buddhist Council held at Vaishali, dissenters asserted that they would not regard all Arhats as perfect. Henceforth, sect after sect emerged from the two broad divisions, Theravada and Mahasanghika, the former having eleven and the latter seven sub-sects. One of the sub-sects of the Mahasanghikas—the Lokottaravadins—deified the Buddha as a super divine being, foretelling the ultimate appearance of Mahayanism.

Generally speaking, Mahayana incorporates the conception of the Bodhisattva, the practice of *paramitas* (six wisdoms), the ten stages of spiritual progress (*dasa bhumi*), the goal of Buddhahood, the conception of *trikaya* and the conception of *dharmasunyata*. The Mahayanists distinguish themselves by saying that they seek the removal of the *kleshavarana* or veil of impurities.

HISTORY OF MAHAYANA

Let us have a flashback of the history of the Mahayana (the greater vehicle) which originated in the early centuries of the common era. On the basis of a statement made by the Buddha immediately after the attainment of Bodhi that he was disinclined to impart the deep philosophical teachings to the people at large, the Mahayanists claim that they have received their doctrines and philosophy directly from the teacher. He communicated the subtle and deeper teachings to a select few—the Bodhisattvas—and the popular ethical teachings to those who were less spiritually advanced, the Sravakas. It has also been claimed that Mahayana must have been in the making for two or three centuries BC but emerged as a system only in the first century.

The Theravada school most probably presents the basic original teachings of the Buddha, but with a good deal of scholastic elaboration. In it there is no belief in God, nor even in a divine absolute; Nirvana is not substance underlying or embracing experienced phenomena; and the Buddha is not regarded as a god. These relatively austere teachings, however, became transformed in the development of the Mahayana from about the first century BC onward. This development had both religious and metaphysical roots. Those Buddhists having faith in the pristine form of Buddhism feel that Mahayanism has taken it far away from the early and true form of Buddhism, and even suggest that Mahayana is not Buddhism but a religion in its own right. Mahayanists would counter that Theravada is one aspect of Buddhism, Mahayana another, and that they are preserving and maintaining the true spirit of the Buddha.

So far as the early history is concerned, it is said that there were Mahayanists at the time of the Buddha's death, but its predominance dates between AD 300 and 500. Mahayana has been generally represented by modern historians as a late form of Buddhism which replaced the austere moral teachings of the founder by an exuberant devotional faith and a virtual pantheon of gods and images, myths and rituals. Others view it as an internally inconsistent metaphysical system which they have sought to interpret and discuss in the light of modern ideas. But actually Mahayana should be understood as the Buddhist notion of universal religions. It is a religion of universal love which is to be systematically pursued by a Bodhisattva.

The most important element in the institutionalization of Mahayana was perhaps the establishment of Buddhist universities. In these centres of learning the elaboration of Buddhist doctrine became the most important goal of monastic life. First at Nalanda and Vallabhi, then at Vikramasila and Odantapuri, Mahayana scholars trained disciples from different parts of the world, and elaborated subtle systems of textual interpretation and philosophical enquiry. The Mahayana scholars played a leading role in the creation of a Mahayana synthesis that satisfied both the intelligentsia and common believers for at least five hundred years.

The Mahayana Philosophy

The Mahayana stands firmly on two feet, Prajna and Karuna, on transcendental idealism and all embracing affection for all kinds of beings, animate as well as inanimate. In Mahayana the attaining of wisdom is for the sake of the practice of compassion.

Mahayanaists seek both *Pudgalanairatmya* (non-existence of the soul) as well as *Dharmanairatmya*, by which they mean that the five elements (*skandhas*) which are the basis for the conception of the *pudgala* (soul) do not exist. In other words, all the elements which compose the worldly objects and beings (dharma) are obliterated. For attaining this goal, Mahayana prescribes the realization of both *Pudgalanairatmya* and *Dharmanairatmya.*

The earliest known exponent of its philosophy were Nagarjuna, Asanga, and Maitreyanath. The western scholars use to say that it was Nagarjuna who brought Mahayana out from the Buddhist church to the external world. Some asserted that he was less the compiler of these Mahayana sutras than the commentator on the sutras which existed before him and which he systematized. It seems that there were two streams of Mahayana in his time. One developed from the bodhisattva point of view, which was held by lay people and originated in north India. The sutras of this stream have Buddha and Bodhisattva as the central idea. In south India developed the philosophical aspect, with the *Prajnaparmitasutra* as central. Although different in origin, both streams of thought have as the central core of doctrine, the vow of the Bodhisattva: to seek enlightenment and to save mankind; in each, in the background, is the idea of emptiness (*sunyata*). When the Bodhisattva Avalokitesvara was engaged in the practice of the deep *prajnaparamita*, he perceived that there are five skandhas and these, he saw, by their very nature to be empty, i.e. neither born nor annihilated.

The Mahayana sutras are written mostly in Sanskrit. The Bodhisattva conception of the Mahayanists led to the introduction of devotion and worship into the religion, bringing in its train a number of divinities who were distinguished as Bodhisattvas, such as Manjushri, Avalokiteshvara, Vajrapani, and Samantabhadra. The belief was that these divine Bodhisattvas had acquired immense merit ensuring them the attainment of *bodhi*, but they refrained from reaching the ultimate because, by becoming Buddha they could no longer exercise *maitri* (love) or *karuna* (compassion) or render service to the world of beings.

The Mahayana was further sub-divided into two schools of philosophy, Sunyatavada (the Madhyamika, of which Nagarjuna was the main exponent) and Vijnanavada of the Yogacara, the main exponent of which was Asanga who was inspired by Maitreyanath, a Bodhisattva.

Decline of Mahayana

Originating in India, the Mahayana spread across Asia, which involved basic shift in doctrine and approach. It is difficult to assess the nature and causes of the decline of Mahayana in India. Although it is possible to argue that the early success of Mahayana led to a tendency to look inward, that philosophers spent their time debating subtle metaphysical, logical, and even grammatical points, the truth is that even during the period of technical scholasticism, constructive religious thought was not dormant. But it may be that as Mahayana became more established and conventional, the need for religious revival found expression in other vehicles. Most likely, Mahayana thinkers participated in a search for new expression, appealing once more to visionary, revolutionary, and charismatic leaders. But the life gradually assumed an identity of its own and this was the Tantric Buddhism. The gradual shift from Mahayana to Tantrayana seems to have gained momentum precisely at the time when Mahayana philosophy was beginning to lose its creative energy. We know of Tantric practices in Nalanda in the seventh century. Nalanda represented the scholastic side of Mahayana, Tantric practices were criticized by the Nalanda scholar Dharmakirti, but apparently were accepted by most distinguished scholars of the same instituion during the following century. We may say that the death of its great patron, king Harsha, in AD 657, signals the decline of Mahayana whereas the construction of the University of Vikramasila under Dharmapala about the year 800 marks the beginning of the Tantric period in Buddhism.

Mahayana in Thailand

From the Mahavamsa, a chronicle of Sri Lanka, as well as Rock Edict XIII of the Maurya emperor Asoka, it is known that after the Third Buddhist Council Asoka sent nine groups of Buddhist missionaries to different countries for the propagation of the Buddha's doctrine. The Thais believe that Sona Thera and Uttara Thera visited Suvarnadvip to preach the Buddhist faith here. Although the identification of Suvarnabhumi is still shrouded in history according to some scholars, the Thai tradition is clear that the name was closely associated with the first phase of introduction of Buddhism in Thailand and this region was located at Nakhon Pathom. The claim of Prince Damrong Rajanubhab that central Thailand was the place where the introduction of Buddhism took place and this was the city of Nakhon Pathom, seems to be logical.

Well before the Thai settled in the central plains of present-day Thailand during the thirteenth century, the Mon population, no doubt taking advantage of a relaxation of Funan supremacy over the Indo-Chinese peninsula, developed a further centre of Indianized culture there. The preeminence of Theravada Buddhism suggested by archaeological remains does not in fact rule out the presence of the Mahayana cult, notably at U Thong (present-day Suphanburi), Khu Bua, or Chedi Chula Pathom at Nakhon Pathom. The city of Si Thap, a commercial staging post between India and the Khorat plateau, acted as a meeting place between Chenla and Dvaravati.

The rise of the fortified cities of the Khorat plateau may also have been linked to intense trading with the plains at a time when the shoreline of the Gulf of Thailand lay further to the north, making access to the sea easier for these parts than it is today. The cities such as Muang Fa Daed, Muang Fang, and Muan Sema were drawn into the orbit of the Mon culture, which may even have extended as far as the fringes of present-day Laos. To the south of the Khu Bua site was another cosmopolitan commercial staging post between India and China providing both a centre of activity for western merchants. This has been judged by the physiognomy and headdress of certain figures represented on buildings. This Khu Bua was a cradle of the flowering of the ancient current of Mahayana Buddhism. Similarly, suggesting a context in which ancient Buddhism was not solidly implanted throughout the Mon world, numerous Bodhisattva images indicate the existence of the Mahayana cult that probably stemmed from contacts with Srivijaya (from the late seventh to the eleventh century) or with Sri Chanasha. Sri Chanasha, an independent state on the edge of the Khmer and Mon worlds, was apparently a centre of Mahayana Buddhism where bronze Bodhisattva images were produced (for example at Ban Fai). Its influence has been traced as far afield as Prakhorn Chai and Thammarat cave. At Khu Bau and U Thong sites or on the fringes of the Mon area, are to be seen figures depicting Avalokiteshvara as well as other Mahayana-inspired figures.

In the beginning of the seventh century, when the rulers of the Shailendra dynasty were consolidating their Sri-Vijaya empire, they conquered several territories including the archipelago of southern Thailand. They were the followers of Mahayana Buddhism which consequently became the accepted religion in the south of modern Thailand. The Sri-Vijaya rulers contributed much to the progress of the Mahayana Buddhism in southern Thailand. Archaeological evidence supports this fact: the great Stupa—the Phra Mahdhatu or Maha-Tat, located in the modern province of Nakon Sri-Tammarat in southern Thailand—indicates the presence of Mahayanism there. There was another stupa in Chaiya, in the province of Surathani. There two Buddhist stupas belonged to the Mahayana style of art. Several Buddha and Bodhisattva images were found in many caves of the Nakon Sri-Tammarat, Trang, Patalung, and Patani provinces and the discovery of these images helped prove the existence of Mahayanism. The image of Avalokiteshvara and large numbers of other deities of the Mahayana pantheon unearthed from there give a clear indication that the people of this region were worshippers of the Mahayana sect and that the seventh century saw the growth and progress of this sect in the religious life of the people of southern Thailand. A large number of votive tablets, referred to as *Phra Pim* (i.e. an object mad of raw clay bearing the figure of the Bodhisattva and the Buddha on its surface) inscribed and dated (between 657 and 757), also suggest the introduction and development of the Mahayana in southern Thailand under the patronage of the Sri-Vijaya rulers.

The Lopbury period witnessed the second phase of the

introduction and development of Mahayana in Thailand. In the beginning of the eleventh century, the reign of the Khmer Suryavarman I marked a turning point in the Kambuja history. The boundaries of the Khmer kingdom were extended far and wide and the lands of the north of the Menam valley were also incorporated. A dated inscription of Saka 944 (AD 1022) found at Lavo or Lopburi, and an undated one from Sal Cau or San Chao in Lopburi, witness Khmer rule there in the eleventh century. Some archaeological evidences also throw light on Khmer rule over Sukhodaya and Sri Sachanlai (Swargalok) in north-central Thailand. During the rule of Suryavarman II (1133 to 1150), Khmer power reached its political and cultural development in Lopburi. Jayavarman VII occupied the entire Menam valley except the Mon kingdom of Haripunjaya. Towards the middle of the thirteenth-century Indraditya became the ruler of the kingdom of Sukhodaya and Khmer supremacy over this region came to an end.

Under the patronage of the Khmer rulers the Mahayana sect began to flourish in several parts of central and eastern Thailand. Many Mahayana temples and images of the Buddha, of Bodhisattvas, and of other Mahayana gods and goddesses were discovered in the provinces of Sakon Nakhon, Nakhon Ratchsema, and Lopburi. A Khmer inscription mentions a decree issued by Suryavarman I, an ardent follower of Mahayanism, that the Mahayana bhikkhus should offer to the king the merits of their piety. The Mahayana sect prospered in Thailand and monuments were built and dedicated to the Mahayana deities and Bodhisattva Avalokiteshvara. The stone temple of Phimai and on the top of the mountain Khao Phnomrung with a large number of sculptural objects found at Lopburi, Phimai, Sri-Top, Buriram and other provinces in the Isan gave an impression of the growth and progress of Mahayana in this region of Thailand. The carved lintels over the doors of the main sanctuary of the Phimai temple indicate that this temple was erected for the Mahayana sect. On the other hand, the Lopburi sculptors created Mahayana Buddha images including standing Avalokiteshvara in *vitarka-mudra* and Maitreya standing, with his thin mustache, no ornaments, short robe and high and full chignon. The style of the Buddha images of the Lopburi school had a single image seated or standing on a pedestal or seated under the Naga. The later part of the twelfth century saw the appearance of a group of Buddhas on the same pedestal. Sometimes, the Buddha is shown under the Naga in the middle, Bodhisattva Avalokiteshvara on the right and the goddess Prajnaparamita on the left.

These epigraphic and archaeological evidences helps us mark that the arrival of the Mahayana sect in Thailand in two different periods—under the patronage of the Sri-Vijaya rulers in the seventh century (southern Thailand) and with the supremacy of Khmer rulers of Cambodia (the Khorat plateau) in the eleventh century.

Mahayana originated and flourished in India and its existence was preserved in Thailand after the pantheon was dying in the land of its origin. The Theravada does not need to mention how a great role it has played in political, religious, social and cultural history of this land of yellow robes, one of the most important Buddhist centres of the world. Yet I think it needs to be reconstructed, how Mahayana once prospered in Thailand, played a vital role here, exerted tremendous influence, and contributed hugely to the religious life of the Thai people.

There must be some conceptual clarifications and some tentative results of studies relating to the origins and development of Mahayana. I would like to suggest that it seems more reasonable, however, to look upon Mahayana as a conception of universal tradition developed within the Buddhist religion. The pioneer work of Chirapat Prapandavidya on the Saba Bak inscription leads us to reconsider Thailand as a strong base of Mahayanism.

Mahayana Buddhism can best be studied today from the Japanese side, for in Japan it is still a living, vital religion and has been studied in all its forms. The Theravada is studied equally, for Mahayana embraces the Theravada and then proceeds along its own lines, being noted for its broad and tolerant spirit and its desire to utilize the best that lies in all Buddhist teachings.

Our concern is that we ought to know all the philosophical attempts made in India, but unfortunately Mahayana is no longer alive in India. Yet its spirit and some of its teachings have indeed been absorbed by other Indian religions and philosophies. Different scholars in dealing with Mahayana have spoken of it as a ritualistic and animistic degeneration of Theravada. Both the Theravada and Mahayana existed in north India and have scattered over all other places in

India and abroad. Probably an organized search for old manuscripts and archaeological explorations would yield rich results and this would certainly be an important basis of our cultural linkage.

SELECT BIBLIOGRAPHY

Dutt, N., *Mahayana Buddhism*, Delhi: Motilal Banarsidass, 1977.

Dutt, N., *Buddhist Sects in India*, Calcutta: Firma KLM, 1977.

Eliade, Mirces (ed.), *Encyclopedia of Religion*, vol. 2, New York: Macmillan & Free Press, 1987.

Kalupahana, J.A., *A History of Buddhist Philosophy*, Honolulu: University of Hawaii Press, 1992.

McGovern, W.M., *An Introduction to Mahayana Buddhism*, Varanasi: Sahitya Ratan Mala, 1968.

Mishra, B.N., *Nalanda*, vol. II, Delhi: B.R. Publishing, 1998.

Suzuki, B.L., *Mahayana Buddhism*, London: George Allen & Unwin, 1988.

The Way of Life and Literature of the Tai Khamti of the Lohit Riverine in Arunachal Pradesh

PRAKONG NIMMANAHAEMINDA

I have had the opportunity to visit the Indian communties of Tai origin on three occasions. The first was during a trip to Assam in 1985, as a member in a party of nineteen scholars led by Kraisri Nimmanahaeminda, who was interested in Tai history and culture and had played an active role in promoting studies in this area. On the trip, which lasted eight days, we were able to join in the *Mae Dum Mae Phi*, a restored sacrificial rite for the ancestors and city spirits. We also visited the Tai Ahom, Tai Rong or Tai Turung, Tai Aiton and Tai Phake villages. The second trip took place in 2000 when I was accompanied by Professors Siraporn Na Thalang and Sukanya Sujachaya of Chulalongkorn University. We were invited to participate in a celebration of the 770th anniversary of Sua Ka Pha, the founder of the Ahom kingdom. This was a grand celebration attended by thousands of participants, in which two events were organized to mark the occasion: an academic conference and traditional festivities. I gave a brief lecture on the similarity of the belief systems of various Tai groups. After that celebration, the next opportunity to visit the Tai Ahom, Tai Aiton and Tai Phake villages, and to visit the Tai Khamti groups, came in March 2006. On this trip there were five members in our group: Suchitra Chongsathitwattana, Siraporn Na Thalang and Sukanya Sujachaya from the Faculty of Arts, Chulalongkorn University and Prakai Nimmanahaeminda from Chiangmai Rajabhat University.

This paper will outline the way of life and literature of the Tai Khamtis who live in the Lohit basin, Lohit District, in Arunachal Pradesh.

ORIGINS, SOCIETY AND WAYS OF LIFE OF THE TAI KHAMTIS OF LOHIT RIVERINE

The Tais who call themselves 'Tai Khamti' possess a language and culture that are similar to those of the Tai or Tai Loang in Myanmar, the Dehong Autonomous Prefecture of China, and Tai Yai in Thailand. The majority of the Tai Khamtis now reside in India and Myanmar. In India, they are found in the states of Assam and Arunachal Pradesh. The group that will be discussed in this paper live along the Lohit river in Lohit district, Arunachal Pradesh.[1]

The ancestors of the Tai Khamtis migrated from the area called Khamti Luang or Bor Khamti in the north-western part of Myanmar, at the headwaters of the Irrawady River. The biggest town of this area is known as Pu Tao or Pu ta-o in Burma while the Tai call it Man Teur, or Man Pa Teur, which means southern village. At present, this town is located in the Singpho state of Myanmar. The Tai Khamtis migrated to India in successive waves between 1750 and 1850 (see Nang Yikham Gogoi, 2006). Initially, they settled down in the plains of the Tengpani River. After a Singpho invasion they made a retreat across the Brahmaputra River and captured the town of Sadiya from a Tai Ahom ruler with the title Khawa Gohain. The Tai Khamti leader who replaced him adopted the local title of Gohain and passed it down to his successors as their family names. This is evident from the name of Chau Khammun Gohain, a son of the last Tai Khamti Ruler, who is now 80 years old. Many explanations have been put forward for the Tai Khamti migration to India, which range from the Burmese invasion to internal conflict among various Tai groups. At present, the majority of the Tai Khamtis reside in the Lohit and Changlang districts of Arunachal Pradesh, and the Lakhimpur, Dhemaji, and Tinsukia districts of Assam.

There are numerous speculations concerning the origin of the name of Tai Khamti.

1. Khamti is a compound word. 'Kham' means gold while 'Ti' means a place (Tai Yai people pronounce the (th) sound as (t)). The land of gold is obviously their homeland, Khamti Luang or Bor Khamti town in Myanmar.
2. Alternately, Kham means to adhere to or to stick to, and 'Khamti' or 'khamthi' means to stick to a place or country,

which suggests the people's close tied to their homeland. Lila Gogoi explains that in the past when the Shan state was invaded by a Tibetan army, a Tai king by the name of Sam-Lung-pha drove it back and closed the Naikhoma pass of the Padkai Ranges forever, restoring peace and allowing the Tai to live peacefully for a long time after that.

3. Khamti is a royal title of subordinate rulers given to them by the sovereign of Mung-kang (Gogoi 1971: xxxiii).

Lila Gogoi states that we can presume the first and third versions and explains that the Mao Luang Kingdom was full of precious ores such as silver, gold, and iron. She mentions a legend which says that there was a heavenly tree full of gold in Bor Khamti (Gogoi 1971: xxxiii–xxxiv). Our group found that this legend is still popular among the Khamtis. One Chau Pha in Impong village narrated the same legend to our party.

The Tai Khamti of Lohit are an agrarian society whose members earn their living from rice cultivation, forestry, trade, and government service. Many of them are well educated, and have a good knowledge of English. Those with means prefer to send their offspring to schools in Shillong and Darjeeling. There are presently a number of people of Chau Pha rank, a group of high-rank royal descendants of previous kings. Apart from Chau Pha Khammun Gohain, who is a son of the last king of the Tai Khamti, our party met three other Chau Phas. With the exception of Chau Pha Khammun, other Chau Pha and royal descendants adopt the last name of 'Namsom'. Chau Pha Navin of Man Kheram explained that this was the name adopted by a Chau Pha who, upon arriving at the Tengpani River, halted his army, performed a divination in which he drank water from the river, and found it to be 'Som' or sour. The name is probably an equivalent to 'Nam Som' (...) in Thai. It is noticed that there are different Romanized versions for this word; it was written either as Namshum or Namsom.

A last name is 'Phan' in Tai Khamti. Most last names generally come from the names of a town, village, and river, for example, Meungpong, Manpung, Mantao, Manjae, Saensap, Manjai, Nanam, Namsaeng, etc.

The Tai Khamti place significance on seniority and masculinity as are evident in the kinship terms which clearly distinguish offspring by the order of their birth for both male and female. It is customary for men to eat before women at meal times. Men are responsible for work that requires strength, while women do household chores and cloth weaving. Tai Khamti women still weave and make their own clothing. The well-to-do families usually build very large houses with hardwood, while the poor build their houses with bamboo. Tai Khamti houses are specially clean and neat.

The Tai Khamtis are a rice-eating people who prefer rice that is less sticky while reserving glutinous rice for making desserts. Their food is a combination of dishes that are similar to those of other ethnic Tai groups and Indian-influenced dishes. Like all Indians they drink tea.

Like the Singpo, the Tai Khamti people are Hinayana Buddhists. However, spirit shrines can still be seen outside houses in some villages. Boonyong Kedtate has mentioned that the Tai Khamtis have a number of spirits or *nats* whom they worship and propitiate for their protection, general welfare, and cure from illness and evils (Boonyong Kedtate 1998: 160). To this day, the Tai Khamtis uphold a tradition of attending sermons at a temple during the Buddhist Lent period. Old people still go to meditate and spend the night at a village temple on Buddhist holy days. Many people stated that they had visited the four holy places of Buddhism in India. They use the word Jong to refer to a Buddhist temple and the word Chau Phala or Phala Chau to refer to the Lord Buddha and Buddhist images. The word 'Phala', which is also used for deity, is probably a derivative of 'Phra'. The Tai Khamtis call a Buddhist monk Mun Chau or Chau Mun, a derivative of 'Bun Chau' and 'Chau Bun'. Since there is no 'b' sound in Tai Khamti, they pronounce the words which begin with a 'b' sound in Thai language with the 'm' sound. They call a Buddhist novice 'Chau Saang' and a nun Yasi or Yasae. Tai Khamti nuns wear pink or orange robes, similar to those of Burmese nuns. Apart from reciting Buddhist precepts to laymen, the monks deliver sermons which can be general moral teachings, or excerpts from Buddhist texts, especially the *Abhidharma*. The monks do not preach the Jatakas or Dharma tales which are the specialties of the Jalae or Mor Leek. The reading of Jataka stories or Dharma tales by a Jalae or Mor Leek is referred to as Hor Leek; the word 'Leek' is a derivative of a Pali word 'Likha'. Apart from Hor Leek, a Jalae also leads the congregation in general chanting and the conduct of ritual. Jalae are usually the learned members of the community and their roles are similar to those of the Tai Myanmar and Thailand. Some Jalae are also poets or Chau Mor. The Tai Khamtis are dedicated to merit *orious* activities. Members of Chau Pha rank usually have a religious building constructed as in remembrance of a deceased sibling or relative. For example, Chau Pha Khammun had a stupa, a Buddhist temple, and a bridge built and dedicated to the Buddha in memory of his dead son. Chau Pha Meohu also had a religious building constructed for his dead son. The Tai Khamtis reserve high reverence to Uppakutta, and often have an image of this Buddist monk placed in Buddhist temples and on river banks, in the belief that this practice will bring rain, fertility, and protection to a community. Moreover, they also believe that certain Buddhist images are sacred and can grant people their wishes. One such image is the Chau Phala Sutong Pae at Jong Impong.

The Tai Khamti observe a lunar calendar. Most festivals are religious. They include for example, the Songkran festival held on the fifth lunar month; the Visakhapucha festival is held in the sixth month. The seventh month is the beginning of a rice cultivation cycle. The Khao Wa (the beginning of the Buddhist Lent) is held in the ninth month, and the Ok Wa (the end of the Buddhist Lent); and the Poi Kathing or Kathin merit-making festival of Thailand is held in the eleventh month. Poi Sum Fai or Poi Mai Kor Sum Fai festival is held in the third month as an offering to the Buddha. Wai Thart or pagoda worship and Vessantara Jataka recitation festivals are held in the fourth month.

Most Tai Khamti words are similar to the language of the Tai or Tai Yai who live in Myanmar, Thailand and China. Some of the words are pronounced differently.

CHARACTERISTICS AND FUNCTIONS OF TAI KHAMTI LITERATURE

As the Tai Khamtis have their own script, they have not only an oral but also a written literature. Tai Khamti letters are similar to those of the Tai Yai. It should be noted that when they write Pali words the Tai Khamtis use a different set of letters, which are probably

Mon letters because there are many similarities between these and those of the Lanna Akson Tham, derived from the Mon script.

According to the author's present data, Tai Khamti literature can be categorized as follows:

1. *Creation myths.* These are myths about the origin of the earth and the ruling class in which some motifs are similar to Tai myths in Myanmar, Thailand and in Dehong, China and to the myths in the Ahom Buranji of the Tai Ahom. The Lengdon and Khun Lu Khun Lai myths are also similar among these Tai groups. I agree with Nang Yikham Gogoi that the Tai Khamti and other Tai groups used to believe in gods. Anyhow, the creation myth of Tai Khamti is influenced by Buddhist literature, such as the story of the enormous fish and the story of Khun Phees and Nang Phees who came down from Maung Phee to eat the fruits of the soft earth. There are also tales of heros which reflect the Tai Khamti ethnic identity and the close relationships among various Tai groups.
2. *Didactic literature.* Examples of this genre are the Lokaniti poems and the Pu Sorn Larn (words of teaching from a grandfather to his grandchildren).
3. *Hindu-influenced literature.* This group consists of the *Ramayana* and *Mahabharata* epics, especially the story about the sixth reincarnation of Visnu, Parasuram, which contains the origin myths of the name of Lohit River and Parasuram Kund in Arunachal Pradesh. Chau Pha Khammun, who as a former member of the house of representatives had been quite popular in politics, seems to be well versed in Indian literature and has an English translation of the *Bhagavad Gita* in his house.
4. *Chronicles and laws.* This category of literature is in the possession of the elite group of Chau Pha and not the temple or commoners. Chronicles are documented accomplishments of the royal families; the laws pertain to rules and regulations essential for the role of the Chau Pha as regulator of social order and adviser to the people. Chau Pha Navin of Man Kheram village showed our party three of his manuscripts. The first is a chronicle of his ancestors, the second a book of laws, and the third, the book of *Vinaya* (Buddhist discipline).

5. *Buddhist-influenced literature.* Buddhism has been crucial in the creation and continuity of the Tai Khamti literature. A large amount of written literature is related to Buddhism.

Like the Tai Lue, Tai Khuen, Tai Yai, Laotians and Thais in northern Thailand, the Tai Khamtis have a long tradition of presenting copies of Buddhist texts to temples. This practice is known as Lu Leek. 'Lu' means merit making while 'Leek' means books and is known among Tai Lue, Tai Khuen, Loatians and Thais in northern Thailand as 'Tan Tham'. People may copy the texts in their own handwriting, or ask others to do it. Numerous Buddhist texts were kept in each Tai Khamti *jong* or temple that the author visited. Each copy of the text is sewn to a special piece of cloth designed to wrap the text after use. On the first page is the name(s) of the text's creator(s) and the objectives of such dedication, which is normally to gain merit for a deceased ancestor or a sick relative. It is normal to find a written wish for a good existence for the ancestors and for their own entrance to heaven and achievement of Nirvana. These offerings are usually copies of sophisticated Buddhist teachings from the *Apidharma* and various Jataka stories from the *Tripitka*. Some texts are folk Jataka derived from local folk tales, such as the Alaung Hoi Khao (Sang Thong), Nang Sipsong (Rotthasen Jataka), Alaung Khao Hom (very similar to the Suthon Jataka), and Tao Kham (Suwan Katjachapa). There are also many other stories from the folk tales, for example, about the Ngu Puak (white snake), Palilai elephant, and Nu Puak (white rat). From my observation of the readings of these stories by the Jalae of Jong Phanaeng and Jong Wengko temples, the texts used in the readings were written in verses similar in style to Rai (. . . .) in Thai poetry. After each reading, the texts, considered sacred, were folded and wrapped in cloth wrappers. Before returning the texts to their places the Jalae would raise them to touch his head in reverence.

Buddhist texts are generally created as an offering to Buddha, a deceased relative, or a temple to accompany a certain request. The texts are carefully selected to suit the creator's objective, for example, to seek profound wisdom one would make an offering of the Chau Maho (Mahasatha Jataka tale) and Chau Sang Nagasin Kab Phamaling Hor Kham

(Milindapanha or The story of Nagasen and King Milinda). Both texts are popular offerings by children of school age who want to be smart and get a good grade. A Tai Khamti policeman revealed that he was not very smart at young age, but after presenting these two texts to the monks his performance had significantly improved. If a recovery from sickness is sought, the Susirakhan and Sang Phaku texts are offered, and if one wishes for a child, the *Pitaka* Khao Tong Chang is chosen. A presentation of Buddhist text(s) to a temple is ceremoniously carried out by placing the text(s) on a tray which holds flowers, popped rice, pencil, book, threads and needles. The threads represent longevity and the needles represent sharp wit and intelligence.

Apart from its educational role, Tai Khamti religious literature serves certain psychological functions, such as providing happiness and confidence. The practice also enhances children's connection with Buddhism, Buddhist texts, and the merit-making tradition of offering texts to Buddhist temples. The Jong Phanaeng temple holds a text entitled *Dharma Sangkhani* which is believed to be brought into India from the town of Khamti Luang more than 200 years ago. The cloth wrapper of this text is replaced every year. As the head of the temple was away on the day we visited the temple we did not get to examine it. It can be said that this particular text does not only play important role in the continuity of Buddhism, it also represents the priceless and unique cultural heritage of the Tai Khamtis.

6. *Oral tradition.* Tai Khamtis are rich in oral traditions such as folktales, proverbs, riddles, lullabies, children's songs, and song duels between males and females. A large number of Tai Khamti folktales and proverbs are more or less similar to those of the other Tai groups like the Tai Lue, Tai Khuen, Laos and Thai.[2]

Song artists are known as Chau Ooy Kham; Contemporary Tai Khamti songs consist of classical songs, newly composed, and Assamese songs.

Among the many folk songs that villagers of Man Saensap sang for us, the author was most impressed by a song written many years ago to praise the magnificence of Vesali, the Tai name for Assam which is the homeland of the Tais. The song describes Vesali as 'Saen Longnum' or extremely beautiful. A line in the song that still lingers in my memory stated, 'Jong Ko Yang, Phala Ko Yang, Tala Ko Yang' which means that temples, Buddha images and Buddhist teachings still exist in the land.

Much Tai Khamti literature is more or less similar to that of the other Tai groups as well as to the Thai literature in Thailand. Some of it is taken from Buddhist texts, while some comes from the Panyasa Jataka (a collection of Jataka tales written by scholars in northern Thailand), traditional folk tales. Didactic literature is very popular among many Tai groups and many versions of the same themes can be found in Laos, Thailand, Sipsongpanna and China. These literatures are comprehensive evidence of the long established contacts between Tai Khamti and other Tai groups. The fact that the Tai Khamtis reside in India makes the Indian influence on their literature more prominent than the literature of other Tai groups.

In a textbook on the Tai Khamti language written by Chaukhouk Manpoong, the author has incorporated many traditional tales and interesting facts about the Tai Khamti culture in an attempt to disseminate Tai Khamti cultural heritage and literature to young people.

Before our departure, a Tai Khamti family invited us to their home to watch a VCD entitled 'Nang Khedla Kham'. Considering that the 'e' sound in Tai Khamti language is equivalent to the ia sound in Thai, the author initially thought that the VCD would be a story about a species of a small green frog. Even after it was explained that 'Khedla' is a type of a tiny fragrant flower, we still could not guess the content of this VCD. It turned out to the tale of the Pikun Thong movie made in Thailand; the only difference was that the Thai actors now spoke fluent Tai Yai. Pikun Thong as well as many other Thai folktales, both old and new, produced as television series and major films, are widely distributed among the Tai Khamti groups as well as in Myanmar and other regions where Tai Yai is spoken. In this modern age of globalization Thai television series with Tai soundtracks have travelled from the Myanmar Shan state across the borders to Assam and Arunachal. With modern technology Thai folk tales and Thai literature has now reached wider audiences among the Tai groups in India who can still speak and understand Tai language.

Acknowledgements: This article would not be possible without the generous assistance of Chowna Mein, Minister of Education, Arunachal Pradesh, who invited our party to visit the Tai Khamti villages. Throughout our stay Chowna Mein provided valuable guidance and facilities for our research. We also met with other academicians, Chau Phas, monks, and local scholars in the villages of Man Chaokham or Man Chongkham, Man Impong, Man Kheram, Man Phanaeng, Man Momong, Man Wengko, Man Mo, and Man Saensap. We express out gratitude to Chowna Mein and his family for their kindness, and to the scholars and villagers in all Tai Khamti villages for their warm welcome and cooperation throughout the period of the visit.

NOTES

1. Established in 1986, Arunachal Pradesh is the 24th state of India. The word 'Arunachal' is a derivative of 'Arun' which means dawn and 'Achala' which means immobile, a reference to a mountain. 'Arunachal' thus means 'land of the mountains of dawn'. The extended mountain ranges of Arunachal Pradesh are lush with greenery throughout the year. The state borders Assam in the south, Nagaland in the south-east, Myanmar in the east, Bhutan in the west and the People's Republic of China in the north. Arunachal Pradesh is the least populated state in India. With a total area of 83,743 km, it had a population of 1,091,117 in 2001, an average of 13 people per km (it was 7 people per km in 1981). Abounding in majestic mountains, rivers, and lush forest, it is a highly fertile and prosperous state. The thirteen tribes of Arunachal Pradesh, which scattered among different villages, can be categorized by their belief systems into three main groups:

    1. *The Buddhists.* There are two sub-groups of the Tibetan Mahayana Buddhists, the Mongpa and Sherdukpens who live in the Tawang and West Kamenge districts, and the Hinayana Buddhists such as the Singpho and Tai Khamti tribes.
    2. *The Animists.* This group believes in the gods attached to the primary features of their natural surroundings for whom they occasionally perform animal sacrifice rituals. Examples of this animist group are the Apatani and Mishmi tribes.
    3. *The Hindus.* These comprise groups like the Wansho and Noctes tribes.

2. See for more details and examples in various articles, such as, 'A Glance of the Tai Khamtis, their Scripts and Literature' by C.N. Lungking, 'Origin of the World & the Tai Khamtis, A Tai Khamti Folktale' and 'Sangken' by Nang Tertia Namshum Sandhu, and 'Folk Tales of Tai Khamtis of Arunachal Pradesh, a Brief Comparative Analysis with their Counterpart in South-East Asia and Southern China' by Nang Yikham Gogoi.

SELECT BIBLIOGRAPHY

Banchob Bhandumetha, *Kale Mantai*, Bangkok: Satrisarn Publishing House, 1961.

———. *Kale Mantai in the Shan State*, Bangkok: Prakaipruek Press, 1983.

Boonyong Kedtate, 'Loh Lum Nam Lohit Liab Cheewit Tai Khamti', Mae Kam Phang Press, 2003.

———. 'Some Aspects of the Thai Khamtis Socio-Cultural Traits', in Shalardshai Ramitanondh, Virada Somswasde, Renu Vichsilpa, eds., *Tai*, Toyota Foundation, 1998.

C.N. Lungking, 'A Glance of The Tai-Khamtis, their Script and Literature', *Buddha Mahotsva 2006*, Chongkham: Print Book Centre, 2006, pp. 12-18.

Chowdhury, J.N., *Arunachal Panorama: A Study In Profile*, Delhi: Himalayan Publishers, 1996.

H. Kri, *Parasuram Kund (A Complete Guide for Visitors)*, Tinsukia: Print & Book Centre, 2006.

Krungthep Turakij, 19th year, issue 6417, Tuesday, 18 April 2006, 'Chud Prakai Parithat' column.

Lila Gogoi, compiled, *The Tai Khamtis of the North-East*, New Delhi: R. Kumar, 1971.

Manpoong, Chau Khouk, 'Buddhism as it is Practised by the Khamtis and Singpho of Chongkham Namsai Area', in *Buddha Mahotsva 2006* Chongkham: Print Book Centre, 2006, pp. 43-9.

Mein, Chowna, *To The Land of Tai Khamtis of Myanmar*, Dhemiji: Chumphra Publication, 2005.

Prakong Nimmanahaeminda, 'Recording a Visit to Pay Respects with our Tai Ahom Brethren', *Phasa Lae Wannakhadee Thai Journal*, 2, 3 December 1985.

Puspadhar Gogoi, *Tai of North-East India*, Dhemiji: Chumphra Publishers, 1996.

Sumitra Pitipat, et al., *The Tai Community in Northern Burma: Southern Shan State, Mandalay Region and Khamti Luang*, Bangkok: Thammasat University, 2002.

Tertia Namshum Sandhu, 'Sangken and Origin of the World & The Tai Khamtis: A Tai Khamti Folk Tale', in *Buddha Mahotsva 2006*, Chongkham: Print Book Centre, 2006, pp. 9-11.

Yikham Gogoi, 'Folk Tales of Tai Khamtis of Arunachal Pradesh: A Brief Comparative Analysis', *Buddha Mahotsva 2006*, Chongkham: Print Book Centre, 2006, pp. 32-42.

Tai Communities in India: Historical Background and Present State

J.N. PHUKAN

IDENTIFICATION

India is home to a little more than two million people of Tai origin. This number is only a fraction of the total population of the country. Grouped into seven communities, the Tai have been living for several hundred years in the eastern parts of the states of Assam and Arunachal Pradesh, and in certain small pockets of Manipur. In Assam and Arunachal Pradesh, they bear a recognizable identity with 'Tai' prefixed to their local names, and also possess identifiable traits of Tai culture and language besides having their own historical writings and tradition which they share with other Tai outside India. As for Manipur, at present the identification of the Tai there is somewhat hazy.

The Tai of Assam and Arunachal Pradesh taken together constitute six communities, the Ahom (Tai-Ahom), Aiton (Tai-Aiton), Khamti (Tai-Khamti), Phake (Tai-Phake), Khamyang (Tai-Khamyang), and the Turung (Tai-Turung).

The Ahoms constitute the predominant Tai group in India. They are settled mainly within the political boundary of Assam. They number approximately two million—this estimate is based on several sources as no population census has been done on a community basis. The Ahom are spread over the seven Upper Assam districts, Lakhimpur and Dhemaji on the north bank, and Dibrugarh, Tinsukia, Sivasagar, Jorhat, and Golaghat on the south bank of the Brahmaputra. They are also found in certain pockets of Sonitpur, Karbi Anglong, Nagaon, and Marigaon districts, and in the city of Guwahati, the capital of Assam. However, the core area of the Ahom population is the former Sivsagar district. Since they have been wet-rice cultivators, they occupy the low-lying areas of the Buri-Dihing,

Disang, Dikhow, Jhanji, Dhansiri, Subansiri, and other tributaries of the Brahmaputra.

The Khamtis, who 'call themselves Tai or Tai Khamtis denoting that they belong to the Tai race' (*Gazetteer of India*, Arunachal Pradesh, Lohit District, ed. S. Dutta Choudhury, 1978: 93) number over 10,000 and are living both in Assam and Arunachal Pradesh. But the majority of them are living in the Namsai (15 villages) and Chowkham (12 villages), the two areas on the bank of the Na-Dihing and the Tengapani rivers in Lohit District of Arunachal Pradesh, where they are an affluent community. During the 1880s the British officials recorded 5 villages in the Tengapani valley, and 9 villages in the Na-Dihing valley (Michel, Report, 141-4). In 1894, J.F. Needham, the Assistant Political Officer of Sadiya recorded about 2000 Khamtis in Sadiya.

The Phakes numbering about 3,000 are spread over in nine villages: Nam Phake near Naharkatiya Town, Tipam Phake near Jaipur (both in Dibrugarh district); Bar Phake, Maan Maw, Nong Lai, Maan Lang, Mong Lang, Migam and Pha Neng near Margherita in Tinsukia district. All Phake villages are located on the Buri-Dihing river. A few Phake families are settled in the Namsai area in Arunachal Pradesh.

The Aitons number about 3,000 and are also spread over nine villages. Of these, five are in Karbi Anglong, three in Golaghat District of Assam, and one village in Lohit district of Arunachal Pradesh. These villages are Ahomani, Banlung, Balipathar, Chakihola and Kaliyani in Karbi Anglong District, and Borhola, Dubarani and Tangani in Golaghat District of Assam, and Jonapathar in the Lohit District of Arunachal Pradesh.

The Khamyangs number about 7,000 and are spread over three districts. The villages of Salapathar, Disangpani, Bargaon, and Rahan Pathar in Sivasagar District; Betani, Na Shyam, and Borhola villages in Jorhat District, and Rajapukhari village in Sarupathar area in Golaghat District. There are two Khamyang villages near Margherita in Tinsukia District. They are Pawoi Mukh and Alu Bari.

The Turung number less than 3,000. The Turung villages are Bar Pathar and Beleng near Barpathar in Golaghat district; Balipathar in Karbi Anglong district; and Pathar Gaon, Tipamiya, Pahukatiya and Abang Gaon in Jorhat district.

As for the Tai in Manipur, they are commonly known as Kabaw, or Kabaw Shan. Kabaw is applied to the Tai as because they originally came from the Kabaw valley on the Chindwin or Ningthi River in Myanmar, and known to the Manipuris as Kabaw Shan. The British officials in the late nineteenth century identified them as Shan. Today, however, the same people, hesitate to identify themselves as Kabaw Shan. I have made two trips to Khrukhul, a village whose inhabitants were recorded as Shan and their language as Shan (Tai). Very recently, the Centre for Manipur Studies in the Manipur University, Imphal, has published a small work by N. Debendra Singh. In Annexure 1 Singh has given a list of different Shan families who came to Manipur at various times. According to this list, the inflow of Shans from the Kabaw valley began in the early sixteenth century and continued until about 1750. These Shans were settled in the Kabaw Leikai zone close to the capital. After 1891, the British administration declared this a 'British Reserved Area', and the people were evacuated from it. They went to different places to settle. Today these supposed Shans deny any knowledge of Shan and do not know that they were called Kabaw Shan or Shan; instead they are eager to call themselves Meitei, an indigenous term applied to the plains Manipuris. In the official records they are

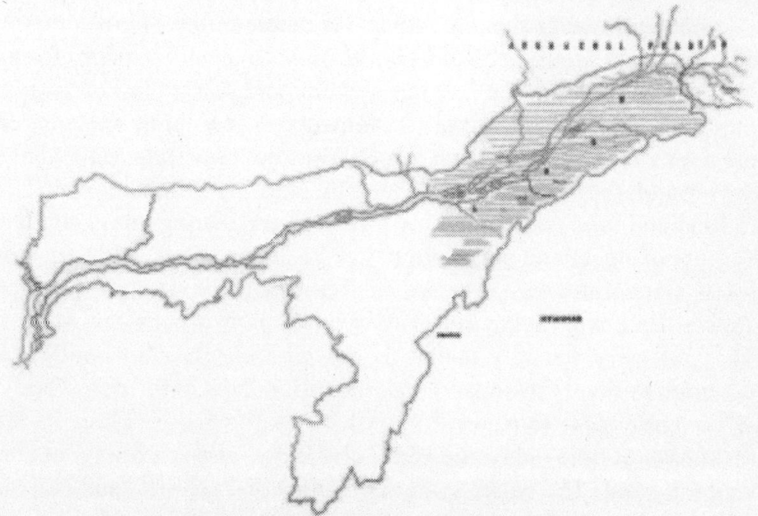

Map of Assam showing Tai Communities

classed under *Loi* (a lower caste), and they do not like to identify themselves as Kabaw Shan, although in the common parlance the Meitei refer to them as Kabaw.

The Indian Tai communities represent the extreme western section of the very widely scattered Tai people who extend from the Hainan Island in the east to the Brahmaputra Valley in the west, and from Guangzi Province of China on the north to the extreme southern point of Thailand. Their westward movement across the rugged terrain of the Upper Irrawady and the Upper Chindwin river basins to reach the Brahmaputra valley as early as the beginning of the thirteenth century itself speaks of the vigour and energy characteristic of the Tai race. Like other Tai, these Tai carried with them their language, culture, and beliefs, in different directions in the mainland South-East Asia; so also the Ahom carried with them their language, culture, belief system, and other Tai traits to north-eastern India.

According to David K. Wyatt, 'the most obvious characteristic that serves to identify the Tai as a separate people is their language' (1984: 2). Originally, all the Indian Tai communities had been Tai speakers, although all of them do not now speak it. But all the groups have a written literature in Tai. The Ahoms possess a very rich treasure of literature that deals with a variety of subjects; all written in the archaic Tai script.

Apart from language, the Indian Tai communities share common cultural traits with other Tai in South-East Asia and southern China in material spheres, the kinship system, and also in belief-system and practices. All have their settlements in low-lying wetlands in the river valleys; they lived in piled houses built several meters above the ground; they used to till the land by employing the male buffalo. In food and food habits they were very liberal, eating things that the neighbouring Hindu population would abhor. They showed preference for glutinous varieties of rice, for duck, and for bamboo shoots. Rice wine (*nam lao*) was very common among the Ahoms. They are very strongly bound by the *pii-nong* (brother bond) that determines family, clan, and social relationships in the community. A common *dam* (ancestral spirit) binds the whole clan. In the reckoning of time—day and year—the *lak-ni* system of sixty cycles was followed. The belief system includes *phii* (spirits) such as the *phii pha* (sky spirit), *phii naam* (water spirit), *phii tun* (tree spirit), *phii then* (forest spirit), *phii phai* (fire spirit), *phii ruen* (house spirit), and *phii baan* (village spirit). These *phii*s are propitiated by rituals including offerings. Tai people remember their ancestors annually and make offerings to them, praying for blessings. All the Indian Tai communities claim that they originally belonged to Mong Mao, or Mong Mao Lung, a Tai state that flourished in Yunnan and northern Myanmar.

THE HISTORICAL BACKGROUND OF THE INDIAN TAI COMMUNITIES

The Ahom

Of the Tai communities the Ahom were the first to arrive in the Brahmaputra valley in the early thirteenth century. From some indirect references in the Ahom chronicles some scholars think that there was migration of Tai to eastern Assam, as early as the eighth century during the heyday of the Nanchao power in south-western Yunnan. This claim has yet to receive support from further serious research. The old historical records of the Ahom are specific that they came directly from Mong Mao, now identified with Ruili in the present Dihong Tai-Singpho Autonomous Prefecture in Yunnan in China. The details of the route the Ahom followed from Mong Mao to the Sivasagar in Assam, as recorded in the chronicles, leave no doubt about this fact. This is thought to be an ancient route that linked China with India and was opened during Namchao times if not earlier. The chronicles record that the Ahoms passed through via Mong Wan, Mong Na, Mong Ti, crossed the Irrawady at Ta Wing Mao opposite Mitkyeina, then passed through Mogaung and Hukwang to arrive at the Khamjang Valley on the south-eastern side of the Patkai Range. After crossing the Patkai by a pass (this pass is now called Pangsu Pass) they reached the eastern extremity of the Brahmaputra valley. Thereafter, following the course of the Buri-Dihing (Nam Jin) and the Dikhow (Nam Sao), they finally settled down in the present Charaideo area by founding a small but independent state. The date of Ahom entry in Assam is 1227.

The leader of these Tai from Mong Mao was Chao-lung Siu-ka-pha, son of Chao Chang Ngeo, a prince of the Mong-Ri Mong-Ram royal line. His mother was a princess of the Mong Mao royal family.

In fact, he was brought up in Keng Sen Mao Lung, and was to succeed the Mong Mao throne, but for the birth of a son to Pa-meo-pung's wife (named Siu-khan-pha). He then left Mong Mao with a large group of people, individuals (*phu*), families (*ruen*) and groups (*pouk*) numbering some 9,000 with three hundred horses and two elephants. There were ministers, officials of rank, and priests bearing such titles as *khun ring, khun-seng, khun ba*, *phu-kin-mong, thao-mong, ru-ring* and *ru-pak*. Thus the first Ahoms brought with them an entire state machinery into the Brahmaputra Valley. Following the Tai living pattern, they settled in the lowlands of the river valleys usually inundated during the rains, where wet rice can be grown easily with the buffalo-drawn plough. Such lands were not as abundant as those of the two local Mongoloid tribes—the Morans and the Borahis—whose number was small who lived on high land above the inundation level and were dry rice cultivators at the subsistence level. The Ahom settlements grew up in the marshy but highly fertile wet land, away from that of the local Borahis and the Morans. The Ahom state was thus a Tai state and was ruled in accordance with Tai systems as in Mong Mao.

Much later, in the beginning of the sixteenth century, this state was expanded by absorbing the neighbouring smaller states, the Chutiya, the Kachari, and the Bhuyan on the north-east, south and west. The power of the Ahom state grew enormously, and by the seventeenth century the whole of the Brahmaputra valley came under its political sway. Other states like Koch Behar and Manipur maintained cordial diplomatic relations with the Ahom. The neighbouring hill tribes too became subservient to Ahom power. This kingdom, called Mong Dun Sun Kham in Tai, was better known as 'Assam'. During the closing quarter of the eighteenth century, the decline of Ahom power set in due to religious sectarianism, internal feuds, and civil war, followed by the Burmese invasions (1816–21), and it came to an end in 1826 following the First Anglo-Burmese War. The Ahom kingdom, ruled by thirty-nine kings of the same dynasty, thus, covers a period of six hundred years.

Ahom rule was remarkable not only for its duration, but also for its achievements. A strong identity and individuality of Assam came to be established. The Ahom gave Assam a stable administration and provided internal security that brought peace and order and socioeconomic development. The Ahom reclaimed the low-lying marshy lands into paddy fields producing abundant rice and other necessities. Their method of wet-rice cultivation was followed by others. They successfully cultivated good relations with the neighbouring hill people as did the Tai elsewhere. Through great sacrifice and dogged tenacity, the Ahom successfully resisted the aggressions of the mighty Mughals and thus saved Assam from being a part of the Mughal dominion. There was great development in almost all spheres of life.

The Ahom rulers were patrons of cultural life of their subjects. They liberally patronized scholars, poets, and artists, and showed keen interest in art and literature. Hinduism flourished in the Ahom kingdom and Hindu preachers received grants of land and men. As a result, many Hindu religious monasteries were founded in various parts of the kingdom. A great number of Hindu temples were built and those in ruins were reconstructed. The Hindu temples now existing in Assam were either built or rebuilt by the Ahom monarchs. The Ahom rulers were also builders of cities such as Garhgaon and Rangpur. The huge burial mounds raised over the vaults of the dead kings at Charaideo in Sivasagar are unique both for their concept and shape. In fact, the majority of the heritage sites in Assam today fall under Ahom heritage sites. Assam is in many ways the creation of Ahom rule.

The Khamti

According to one source, on the dismemberment of the Shan States by Alaungpaya, the Khamtis numbering about a hundred left their homeland in Khamtilong near the source of the Irrawady River and came to the Ahom kingdom some time after 1753. The then Ahom monarch, Siu-rem-pha (Rajeswar Singha), gave them permission to settle in the valley of the Tengapani, a tributary of the Lohit, the easternmost branch of the Brahmaputra. Some time later, 400 more Khamtis migrated from Khamtilong and joined the earlier colonists. During the reign of Chao-pha Siu-hit-pong (Gaurinath Singha, 1780–95), the rebellion of the religious sect called Moamarias caused complete anarchy in Upper Assam, and the king had to leave for Lower Assam. Taking advantage of the breakdown of the Ahom authority, the Khamtis pushed on to Sadiya, and by ousting the Ahom governor of Sadiya, made their chief the governor of Sadiya. The Ahom government had to recognize his authority under the royal authority. However, there had been occasional troubles between the Khamtis and the royal troops. During the period of Burmese occupation of the Ahom kingdom (1819–24), the Sadiya area was placed under the Khamti chief.

When the British occupied Upper Assam, Captain Neufville bestowed the title of Sadiya Khowa Gohain (Governor of Sadiya) on the Khamti chief. About a decade later when Capt. Charlton was placed in charge of the Khamti chief and the Sadiya and Saikhowa districts, he adopted measures that created dissatisfaction among the Khamtis. Considering the unrest of the Khamtis as dangerous, Charlton deposed the Khamti chief. This was followed by serious apprehension of an open revolt of the Khamtis. The revolt of the Khamtis surfaced in January 1839. Supported by the Muluks and Singhos, the Khamtis attacked the British sepoys and their lines. Colonel White and eighty others were killed. However, the Khamtis, fearing severe reprisals, took shelter in the hills. Following this the British authority was firmly established in Sadiya. Some time later, a small body of Khamtis, including their chief who had submitted to the British, were deported to Narayanpur in the present Lakhimpur district, where they are still living. Some years later, the leaders of the revolt prayed for return to Sadiya. On certain conditions, they were allowed to settle near Sonpura, to the east of Sadiya. In 1842, the Khamti territory was incorporated with the rest of Assam.

The Phakes and the Aitons followed the Khamtis along the Patkai route and with the permission of the Ahom king settled on the bank of the Buri Dihing River. The Khamyangs and the Turung were the last Tai tribes to enter Assam at the beginning of the nineteenth century. Numerically these Tai communities were small, but were well-organized under their own chiefs.

PRESENT STATE OF TAI COMMUNITIES: THE PROBLEM OF BEING SMALL

In terms of language, the Ahom today speak not Tai but Assamese, an Indo-European language, and so also the Khamyangs. The

Turungs, however, speak Singpho mixed with Tai, as they lived among the Singphos in the Hukwang Valley in Burma before their migration to Assam. But the Khamtis, Aitons, and the Phakes are Tai speakers. However, all the Indian Tai communities possess literature written in Tai script. The Ahom script is archaic but similar to the script used by the Tai of Mong Mao before the introduction of reform in script by the Chinese government. On the other hand, the scripts of the other Tai groups are quite similar, and mutually intelligible. Certain Ahom letters are identical with those of other Tai groups. No doubt the Ahom do not speak Tai, but their priests, called *mo'* (or *maw*), invariably read or recite chants or *mantras* written in the old Ahom language during worship (*phii/pha*), ancestor rituals (*dam*), *khwan* calling, or such other occasions. Their pronunciation may not be intelligible to Tai speakers due to lack of tone in their utterance. In this sense the Ahom language is not altogether dead.

There is an increasing awareness among all the Indian Tai communities about their language. They are now fully conscious that their language is a cultural continuum and symbol of identity. This has assumed significance in the context of identity crises and the cultural resurgence and assertion of many tribes in India's north-east. Attempts are therefore being made by the Indian Tai communities to retain and revitalize their language despite several obvious deterrent factors. Today, there is a strong movement among the Ahom to revive or revitalize their language. Almost all the organizations are backing this move. Under their pressure, a Diploma Course in Tai-Ahom has been introduced in Dibrugarh University and the Central Tai Academy at Patsaku in the centre of an Ahom priest settlement has been imparting instruction in the Ahom language. For the last several years Ahom is taught at the primary level in 200 schools (with predominantly Ahom students). However, due to several factors, the progress is not very satisfactory. In the same way, other Tai groups are also doing their bit to revitalize the Tai language.

By religion, the Tai barring the Ahoms are Theravada Buddhists. Formerly they received their religious instructions from Burma, and many monks came from that country. For a long time the Burmese Buddhist Temple in Kolkata has been a conduit of Buddhist monks and literature to monasteries in Assam and Arunachal Pradesh. Due to the prevailing political uncertainties in Myanmar and restrictions imposed by its ruling authority, the free flow of monks has recently been greatly reduced. There is a shortage of local monks as well. Yet, the number of Buddhist monasteries in the region is increasing. For instance, within the Guwahati city area alone there are at present five Buddhist temples, for a Buddhist population of barely two thousand. Under the circumstances, monks from other Buddhist communities, particularly the Chakma, are taking charge of many monasteries, while in others local monks are the heads. But there is now increasing contact with Thailand through the World Fellowship of Buddhists and other Buddhists and monks. Buddhists Tai are enjoying increasing contact with Buddhists outside the country.

Today most Ahoms identify themselves as 'Hindu' and are divided into several major sects or orders, each headed by a guru. Of them the Vaishnavite section is more numerous. The 'Hindu' Ahoms follow the Hindu scriptures and perform rituals in accordance with the prescribed rules. But interestingly, excepting a small number, they do not observe the Hindu rites and rituals as strictly as do the caste Hindus—they are liberal about food and drink. However, even today many Ahoms, including members of the priestly families, hold on to their old beliefs and practices. They perform rites and rituals that include ancestor worship (*dam*), *rik khwan* (*hong khwan*); burial of the dead (*moi dam*) and the raising of earthen tumuli over them, weddings in the customary way (*chak long*); and the worship of ancient gods (*phii-pha*) by sacrificing birds and animals. In recent years, there has been an increasing concern to revitalize and re-establish their traditional rites and ceremonies. Thus *me-dam me-phi*, *rik khwan*, *om pha* and other rituals are performed in a big way, in public, when thousands join the function. There is a general feeling among the Ahoms that Hinduism has greatly affected the traditional culture and identity. Hence they are turning towards the older religious practices. Many Ahoms have thus joined a sect called Phra Long (or Phra Along) which they believe to be an ancient cult.

As regards their constitutional position, the Ahoms are an 'Other Backward Class' (OBC), while other Tai groups enjoy the status of Scheduled Tribes. However, the Ahoms are demanding Scheduled

Tribe status, and the move is supported by the state government of Assam.

CONTACT WITH THAI AND THAILAND

The Indian Tai communities are in increasing contact with Thailand. Before 1980, only a few persons from Thailand had visited the Tai of Assam, which was then a restricted area for foreigners. In 1955, Professor Banchob Panthumetha (1920–92) had visited Assam to study Tai language, and wrote about it in *Kale Maan Tai* (A Visit to the Tai Village).

Almost at the same time Sang Pattanothal (1915–86) visited the Tai and published *The Thai-Ahom: Our Blood Brothers* under his pen-name 'Sarnath', in 1954. In January 1985, on the invitation of the Ahom people on the occasion of Me-Dam Me-Phi, a selected group of nineteen Thai scholars, businessmen, and others led by the late Kraisri Nimmanahaeminda, came to Assam and spent four nights among the Tai of Assam. But the First International Conference on Thai Studies held in New Delhi in 1981 (at the initiative of Dr. Sachchidnanda Sahai and his Thai friends) was the first major meeting which a large group of Ahoms attended, and could exchange ideas and information with many Thai scholars. This facilitated personal level contact between Tais in Assam and in Thailand. Subsequent international conferences held in Bangkok, Kunming, London, and Chieng Mai were also attended by Tai scholars from India. These occasions were utilized for interaction and exchange of information and knowledge that surely contributed to strengthen the relations between individuals. On other occasions, too, individuals and groups of Tai from India have visited Thailand. By this time, many Thai academics have become interested in the history, culture, and language of the Tai in India, and scholars from various institutions of higher learning (more particularly from Chulalongkorn, Thammasat and Chieng Mai universities) have made study visits to Assam and Arunachal Pradesh. Dr. Chathip Nartsupha, Dr. Parkong Nimmanahaeninda, Dr. Willaivan Kantitanan, Dr. Rano and several others made several visits for research. Some of them stayed in the Tai villages and collected data. The visits of ambassadors of the Royal Thai Embassy in India to Assam and Arunachal Pradesh were hailed by the Tai people as furthering the bonds of contact. We believe that the groundwork has already been laid for strengthening Indo-Thai relations at the national level. The Tai communities in India are known to academic circles in Thailand and also to some other countries of South-East Asia.

In conclusion, may I be allowed to say that the Indian Tai communities who share a common cultural heritage (including Buddhism), with the Thai of Thailand and of other South-East Asian countries deserve to have a more meaningful role in forging the relations between India and Thailand. But the roles assigned to them must have a positive tone and work in the greater interests of India and Thailand. Individual contacts need to be raised to institutional and international levels. The ICCR must undertake several programmes to serve this purpose.

SELECT BIBLIOGRAPHY

Ahom Buranji, ed. & tr. from original Ahom by Golapchandra Barua, Assam Administration, 1930.

Buragohain, Joya, 'The Aitons in Transition', Ph.D. thesis, Gauhati University.

Buragohain, Pratashlata, 'The Ahom Population of Assam', Ph. D. thesis, Gauhati University, Guwahati, 1998.

Chao-lung Siu-ka-pha, ed. & tr. J. N. Phukan, Romesh Buragohain, and Ye Hom Buragohain, Guwahati, 1998.

Chetia, Satyaneth, *Tai Ahom Marriage*, Guwahati, 2005.

Gazetteer of India, Arunachal Pradesh, Lohit District, ed. S. Dutta Choudhury, 1978.

Gogoi, Bontirani, 'The Turung', Ph. D. thesis, Gauhati University.

Gogoi, Lila, *The Khamtis*, Chowkham, 1971.

Gogoi, Padmeswar, *The Tai and the Tai Kingdoms* (with a Fuller Treatment of the Tai Ahom Kingdom in the Brahmaputra Valley), Gauhati: Gauhati University, 1968.

Gohain, U.N., *Assam under the Ahom*, Jorhat, 1942.

Sharma Thakur, G.C., *The Tai Phakes of Assam*, Delhi, 1983.

Singh, N. Debendra, *Identities of the Migrated People in Manipur*, Imphal, 2005.

Terwiel, B.J., *The Tai of Assam and Ancient Tai Ritual*, 2 vols. 1980-1981, Gaya.

Wyatt, David K., *Thailand: A Short History*, New Haven: Yale University Press, 1984.

Socio-cultural Status of the Tai Communities in India

YE HOM BURAGOHAIN

In India, the communities of Tai origin are confined to the north-east, particularly Assam and Arunachal Pradesh. Altogether six communities are identified as Tai: Ahom, Aiton, Khamti, Khamyang, Phake, and Turung. All of them claim to have come from Mong Mao Lung, an ancient kingdom located in south-western Yunnan and Myanmar. Of these communities, the Ahom or Tai-Ahom were the first to arrive in India in the early thirteenth century. Much later, they were followed by other Tai groups. All of them passed through Mogaung and Hukwang in Myanmar.

The Khamtis came from Khamti-lung in the extreme northern Burma near the source of the Irrawady some time in the middle of the eighteenth century when the Burmese monarch Alaugpaya had broken up the Shan power in Upper Burma. The Aiton came from Aiton, a place situated near Mogaung in Burma, also in the latter half of the eighteenth century. The Phakes came from the Phake-Che-Rin, a place to the east of Hukwang valley in the upper Chindwin region. The Khamyang came from Khamyang, a small valley to the south of the main Patkai range, and the Turung from the banks of the Turung Pani, a tributary of the Chindwin, all in the eighteenth century. Thus the Tai communities have been living in India's north-east for centuries. Excepting the Ahom, who are not Buddhists, the other communities are Hinayana Buddhists. For discussion at this seminar, I have taken up these five Buddhist Tai communities.

BUDDHIST TAI SETTLEMENTS

All the Tai communities, including the Ahom, are valley-dwelling people like other Tai elsewhere. Hence on coming to then Tai-Ahom kingdom, they settled along the river courses. The Khamtis settled in the valley of the Tengapani river, and later some moved to the Na-Dihing valley. The Phakes settled in the upper valley of the Buri-Dihing river. The Aitons and Khamyangs also followed the Phakes, but ultimately moved south and settled in the valley of the Disang and Kakodunga in Sivasagar and Jorhat. The Turungs were brought to Sivasagar by Captain Neufville some time in 1825, and thereafter moved to the Dhansiri valley, and are settled in Golaghat district. Today the Tai Buddhists are spread over several districts of Upper Assam. Below are shown the areas and approximate population of the Tai Buddhist people of Assam and Arunachal Pradesh:

Aiton: 3 villages in Golaghat district: Dubarani, Tengani, Borhola. 5 villages in Karbi Anglong: Banlung (Bargaon), Ahomani, Chaki Hola, Bhitor Kaliyani and Balipathar. Total population: approximately 3000.

Khamti: In Narayanpur area of Lakhimpur: 7 villages: in Chowkham in Arunachal Pradesh: 12 villages (but three villages with other people); in Namsai in Arunachal Pradesh: 15 villages (seven villages mixed with Singpho); Bardumsa: 1 village; Margherita: 1 village; and a few Khamti people in Sadia. Total population: about 10,000.

Khamyang: In Golaghat: 1 village, Jorhat: 3, Sibsagar: 3, Tinsukia: 2 villages; in Arunachal Pradesh: 3 villages. Total population: 7,000.

Phake: In Dibrugarh: 2 villages; Tinsukia: 7 villages; Total population: 3,000.

Turung: In Golaghat: 2 villages; Jorhat: 2 villages; Balipathar: 3 villages; Karbi Anglong: 1 village. Total population: 3,000.

These settlements lie in the interior, away from the settlements of other people. Because of differences in language, religion, and culture the Buddhist Tai have lived in comparative isolation. Roads were practically non-existent and even today many of these villages are not easily approachable during the rainy season. Hence the people of such villages do not enjoy modern amenities like electricity, potable water, medical services, and schools.

LANGUAGE AND LITERATURE

Originally all the Tai groups were speakers of Tai of the Mao Shan variety. However, the Ahoms, Turungs, and the Khamyangs (except a few persons) no longer speak Tai. The Ahoms and the Khamyangs speak Assamese; the Turung speak Singpho mixed with Tai. Only the Khamtis, Aitons, and the Phakes still speak Tai as their mother tongue, which is the same as that spoken in the northern Shan States of Burma, more particularly Shans in the upper region of the Irrawady valley. They find very little difficulty in following Tai spoken by the Shan of Burma or even the Thai of Northern Thailand. This is certainly a welcome situation that can be exploited in the context of India–Thailand relations. On the part of these Tai-speaking communities, it will also be easier to learn Thai.

The Buddhist Tai communities possess a literature written in the original script. Some manuscripts deal with Buddhism and related subjects. The most common Buddhist manuscripts are the Pitakas—*Abhidhamma*, *Suttanata*, *Vinaya*—or their different sections or chapters. The Buddhist Jataka stories and allied subjects form other Buddhist literature. Such literature is basically no different from Thai Buddhist literature and is common to both the Thai of Thailand and other Tai of South-East Asia.

In addition to Buddhist literature there is also a secular literature. This includes chronicles and manuscripts dealing with socio-cultural aspects of the Tai people. Each Tai tribe has its own chronicle giving an account of its origin, history, and movement. The literature includes *Lik Khu Khun* (Genealogy of Kings), *Lik Khu Mong* (Chronicle), *Lik Weichalli* (Account of Burmese Invasion), *Lik Pu Son Lan* (Grandfather's Advice to Grandson), *Lik Tai Khawm* (Maxims and Proverbs), *Lik Hong Khwan* (Calling of Khwan), *Thammast* (Traditional Law), *Lik Hitopatesa (Hitopadesha)*, *Lik Lokasammukdhi* (Rules and Procedures of Death and Disposal), and *Lik Phe* (Divination).

The Tai Buddhist communities are rich in folk literature such as proverbs, maxims, saying, folktales, riddles, and lullabies. The older generation of people very often uses these to convey thoughts and ideas both in public and private conversation. This is a very rich treasure possessed by them. All these are reflections of life and culture of the Tai people in the past. Their past can be reconstructed, at least in part, with the help of these elements of folk literature.

Though the Ahom lost their language many years ago, they still are rich in literature in various subjects. These are assets not only for historians but also for the cultural heritage. The literature of the

Ahoms may be divided into eight sections, chronicles, legends, *Phura long*, *Lakni (Ahom Era)*, Omens and Divination, Ritual and Mantra, Astrology, and Lexicons.

While the Ahom manuscripts are written mostly on *sanchi pat* (*Aquilaria agallocha*), thickly woven *endi* or *muga*, the outer crust of oblong bamboo pieces, those of the Tai Buddhist communities use hand-made paper. The hand-made papers are of two kinds, one smooth, the other thick. The thick variety is used to make accordion-shaped manuscripts that are quite long. Usually all Tai peoples prepared ink from several natural ingredients and used fern pens for writing.

AGRICULTURE

For these valley dwelling people agriculture is the main livelihood. Agriculture always played the most important role in the economy of the Tai people. They were and are even now good wet-rice cultivators usually engaging buffaloes for ploughing. At the present time many have shifted to bullocks. All of them are fond of the glutinous variety of rice and prefer steamed method of preparing rice. They now produce potato, jute, mustard, corn, ginger, turmeric, areca nut, *tokow* (leaves of a variety of palm), bamboo, and sugar-cane. Their agriculture uses the old traditional methods. Implements and tools include wooden ploughs with small iron shares.

RELIGION

Except for the Ahom, the other Tai groups had been Hinayana Buddhists before their arrival in Assam and as such they maintain the religion till today. Every village has a Buddhist temple which is the centre all social and religious activities. It is managed by a Buddhist bhiksu, and religious teaching is imparted. From time to time, elderly persons go to these monasteries and impart advice and also *pancha sila* or *ashta sila*. The temple is the centre of all religious festivities and celebrations. The traditional Buddhist festivals form an inseparable part of socio-religious life. These celebrations are no different from those observed by the Thai of Thailand and other Tai. Among them is the Poi Sangken, an important traditional

Buddhist religious festival of the Tai people. Sangken usually falls in the Tai month of Nuan Ha (the fifth month) but occasionally in Nuan Huk (the sixth) both corresponding to mid April or *Bohag Bihu* in Assam. Mai Ko Sum Phai, or Mai Lum Phai is another traditional festival of Tai in Assam and Arunachal Pradesh. This festival falls in the month of full moon of Nuan Sam (the third). A huge amount of firewood is required for this purpose.

Poi Nuan Huk is celebrated on the Full Moon day in the sixth month marking the birth of Lord Buddha, his attainment of Buddhahood, and his nirvana. Poi Ok Wa is observed by laymen when the Buddhist monks coming out from the three month retreat. In Poi Kathin, elsewhere in the Buddhist world, a robe is donated by laymen in a sort of celebration. On the occasion of the donation of Buddha statue, a celebration known as Poi Lu Phra may be organized. In the same way, other Buddhist festivals are observed by the Buddhist Tai communities of India.

OTHER BELIEFS

The Buddhist Tai communities of India also have more ancient belief system. They believe in *phii nam* (deity of ancestor), *phi huan* (deity of house), *phii nam* (water spirit), *phii nin* (earth god), *phii su mong* (spirit of domain), *phii huen* (house spirit), *phii phai* (fire spirit), *phii thuen* (forest god), and some others. These spirits and gods are propitiated as the occasion demands. For instance, when a person returning from the forest falls ill, it is believed that the forest spirit is offended. So *phi thuen* is propitiated by offering flowers and candles near the forest. The Tai, however, do not consider that such beliefs and practices are affecting their Buddhism.

SOCIAL LIFE

As the Buddhist Tai groups have lived in the interior areas and led a life of isolation away from other people, they have maintained a separate social identity and institutions. Earlier, they married amongst themselves and this too helped them to retain their traditional institutions.

Tai society is patriarchal. It is customary for fathers to make provisions to divide immovable property among their sons before death. Then and now, immovable property is inherited by sons alone. Daughters have no claim on property. To avoid disputes in future, the father makes equal divisions to his sons. The elder sons make separate establishments after their marriage. The parents usually lived with their youngest son until their death. After their death he receives the property left with them.

In rare cases, daughters also receive immovable property. In case there is no son, the daughter who inherits, should look after her parents.

The Tai system of kinship terminology in Assam and Arunachal Pradesh is similar to that of other Tais.

Some common terms are given below:

Father	*po*
Mother	*me*
Grandfather	*pu*
Grandmother	*yaa*
Elder Brother	*pi chai*
Elder Sister	*pi sao*
Younger Brother	*nong chai*
Younger Sister	*nong sao*
Mother's father	*pu nai*
Father's elder sister	*pa*
Father's younger sister	*aa*
Mother's elder's sister	*pa*
Mother's younger sister	*na*

All Buddhist Tai communities follow the traditional way of naming their children. The following are the prefixes that indicate the order of the male and female children. The system is given below:

Birth order	Male	Female
First	Ai	Ye
Second	Ngi	Ee
Third	Cham	Am
Fourth	Chai	Ay

Fifth	Ngo	Ok
Sixth	Nuk	Et
Seventh	Nak	Att
Eighth	Nauk	Ot

The Ahom people too followed this traditional Tai system. Even the Ahom kings also had their children named in such order.

Food and Food Habits

Rice is the staple food of Tai people of Assam and Arunachal Pradesh. They cultivate *Khao Tai* for their consumption. *Khao Tai* is said to have been brought by them from their original home land.

Vegetables form a major part of the diet. Roots and stems of herbs and creepers, as well as edible leaves, are consumed seasonally. Besides these, meat, fish, and eggs are eaten with rice. They also use variety of indigenous spices collected locally such as *kangchang, khikai, hiu, liwai, panang, pakut, pakhoi, paman, samkha,* and mushrooms. Vegetables such as *pakat sum* (sour leafy vegetable): *pakatkat sum, paman sum, na sum* (sour bamboo shoot) *na je* (bamboo shoot keeping in water) and *na hiu* (dried sour bamboo shoot) are preserved. The first two items are prepared during winter and the latter during the rainy season.

Tai women are experts in searching out edible herbs, roots, and creepers from the forest and fields. Tai prefer boiled vegetables to fried ones. Rice, however, can be prepared in many ways. For example, *khao nung* (steamed rice), *khao puk* (sticky rice cake), *piang* (rice cake), *khao tek* (parched paddy), *khao Mao* (flat rice made of parched half boiled paddy) and *khao pong* are the variations on the staple diet.

Dress

In the matter of dress the Aiton, Khamti, Khamyang, Turung women generally wear black *mekhela*, blouse, green *riha* (*nang wat*), red waist band (*sai kap*) and white turban. The *mekhala* (sin) and *riha* (*nang wat*) of Phake women are multi-coloured and they wear white turbans. The men wear multi-coloured *lungis* (*pha noi* or *pha nung*).

BUDDHIST TAI COMMUNITIES AT PRESENT

The Tai communities have long been in India, and India is their homeland. They identify themselves as sons of the soil. However, they have not forgotten their past and are proud to introduce themselves as Tai in the ethnic sense.

At present the older generations of Tai like to hold on to their old customs and tranditions but the transition of customs and tradition is apparent among the younger generation. Several factors contributed to bring this change of the Tai communities: greater contact with non-Tai people in daily life; the opening up of roads to the Tai villages and consequent access to non-Tai people, and schools where Tai boys and girls study with non-Tai students. In the Khamti villages in Arunachal Pradesh and in some villages in Assam, Tai is taught as a language in village schools. However such teaching is yet to be formalized by the government. For formal education Tai children go to schools where the medium of instruction is Assamese, or English, and Tai children mix with other children. There is an increasing frequency of marriage of Tai with non-Tai, and it is affecting their social system. Among other factors, the electronic media like T.V. has an impact on the younger generation. The traditional dwelling house built on piles has now given way to a ground-level house. This has brought a major change in the traditional perception of Tai living space. Such change is inevitable and no society could escape from it. However, it is also creating an awareness among them for the preservation of their language, religion and cultural moorings. Perhaps they will learn more from the Thai people of Thailand as how to sustain themselves in spite of being modern and global. Right now the Indian Tai communities still have many common cultural elements that could be fruitfully used to strengthen relations between India and Thailand. Already many Thai persons from Thailand, either individually or in groups, have visited the Tai villages and enjoyed the warmth of being amongst the Tai.

SELECT BIBLIOGRAPHY

Barua, G.C., ed. & tr. *Ahom Buranji*, Calcutta: Assam Administration, 1930.

Gogoi, Lila, *The Tai Khamtis*, Chowkhamba, 1971.

Gogoi, Padmeswar, *The Tai and the Tai Kingdoms*, Gauhati: Gauhati University, 1968.

Lik Hong Khwan (in manuscript) in Tai Aiton, Tai Khamti,Tai Khamyang, Tai Phake, *Pu San Lan* (in manuscript) in Tai Phake.

Lik Khu Khun (manuscript) in Tai Phake.

Lik Khu Mong (manuscript) in Tai Phake.

Lik Tai Khwam (in manuscript) in Tai Phake.

Pu San Lan (in manuscript) in Tai Khamti.

Shalardchai,Virada Somswasdi and Ranoo Wichasin, eds. *Tai*, Chieng Mai: Toyota Foundation.

Terwiel, B.J., *The Tai of Assam* (2 vols.), Gaya, 1980-81.

———, and Ranoo Wichasin, *The Tai Ahoms and the Stars*, Cornell University: SEAP, 1992.

Thakur, Ganesh Sharma, *The Tai Phakes of Assam*, Delhi, 1982.

Philosophy of Life: Buddhism in Practice Today

(With special Reference to Hinayana School of Thought)

RAVINDRA KUMAR

To make human life worthy, prosperous, and peaceful, different philosophies and thoughts have been propounded through the ages, among which Buddhism occupies a prominent place. This is evident from the fact that seven hundred million people over the world carry out their day-to-day activities on the basis of Buddhist doctrines. The Buddhist community has the fourth place among the major religious communities of the world, after Christianity, Islam, and Hinduism.

In quite simple and clear words, Buddhism consists of that great and all-welfaristic philosophy of life, that Gautama Buddha put forth before world[1] about two thousand five hundred years ago. Its central theme was *karuna* or compassion, a value supplementary to *ahimsa* or non-violence. The individual must live his life in accordance with these principles.

Karuna is not the word for pity, as is generally understood. Like *ahimsa*, it too involves a wider concept. It is, in fact, an abridgement of compassion and friendliness; in it, there is an urge for equality based on affection and friendliness.

Gautama Buddha was fully aware of the situation in which a person desires to control others; he wanted to keep him in higher position in comparison to others. The Buddha, a great *guru* with great mind was also aware that this factor can be responsible for social disintegration. This is why he, having *karuna* in his being, emphasized on equality amongst all human beings, men and women, and with no caste or class barriers between them.

Till the last breath, Gautama Buddha tried to make human beings understand that surety of existence could be possible if the path of equality was followed; progress could be made if the desire of becoming master was relinquished; peace can be achieved if human beings, knowing the reality, control themselves and become compassionate in heart and soul.

Hinayana is one of the prominent schools of thought of Buddhism. Generally, it is believed that Hinayana thoughts are individualistic; the maximum stress is to take a human being towards happiness, prosperity, peacefulness, and ultimately to salvation or *Nirvana*, leaving behind personal suffering, or grief (*dukha*) and creating full understanding and reality of the Four Noble Truths or Arya Satya in him. This is through the unique Eight-fold Path.

Many amongst scholars of both East and West have extended the argument that, because Hinayana philosophy is centred on the individual, it is micro in dimension; and it is for this reason, perhaps, that it has been linked to the world *hina*, which, simple, can be defined as 'small', 'low', or 'less'.

But, in reality, despite being centred on individualism, the message and objective of Hinayana philosophy is not small, its depth cannot be underestimated. Hinayana Buddhism is in fact a good introduction to what the Buddha himself had taught.

Many verses of the *Dhammapada* also clearify the above reality, and the following *pada* demands special attention in this regard:

'Do not forget him for the sake of others, however, great (they are); care for the self first and then adhere to the welfare of all'.[2]

Along with this, other verses may be quoted in support of the argument from the *Pupha Vaggo*, the *Sahassa Vaggo*, and the *Brahmana Vaggo.*

In the 50th verses of the *Pupha Vaggo*[3] Gautama Buddha says: 'A man must look at his own misdeeds or negligence, and not of others' sins or faults; he must not take notice of others' (ill) words.'

Similarly, *Tathagata* (in verses 104 and 105 of the *Sahassa Vaggo*)[4] conveys the message, 'One's own (self) conquered is better than to conquer others. One who conquers himself, and is restrained, is indeed a good person (man) and 'One who conquers himself, he cannot be defeated (even) by a god, by a *gandharva*, or by *mara*, or by Brahman'.

Emphasizing self-purification by self-beginning, Shakyamuni Gautama (verses 158-159 of the *Dhammapada*)[5] says, 'Let (a man) indulge himself first to what is good (act) and then let him teach (the same) to others; doing this, a wise and intelligent one will not suffer. Let him make proper first what he wants to teach others; control himself first before directing others (to do so). In fact, to subdue one's own self is difficult.'

And last, his preaching that 'man is himself his master; no other can be his master; and rare mastership is gained only after sublimating oneself adequately', can also be seen in this very context.[6]

After analysing above verses, what conclusion appears before us? Is the Hinayana philosophy really individualistic or of a micro dimension, or centralized upon the individual? I think not.

In truth Hinayana philosophy was in existence during the time of Shakyamuni Gautama, and much before the emergence of the Mahayana, another prominent branch of Buddhism; then it may not have been known as Hinayana—this term came to light at the time of rise of Mahayana during a broad discourse on Buddhist philosophy, which took place after the *Parinirvana* of Gautama Buddha. Nevertheless, Hinayana was discovered as the rival word by a great intellectual belonging to the Mahayana school of thought. Perhaps that great intellectual meant to downgrade a rival philosophy in comparison to his own views and for this reason he called it Hinayana (lesser vehicle). Even then, Hinayana is not a lesser vehicle; it is important and relevant today.

As is well-known, Gautama Buddha, too, accepted the principle of enjoying or suffering the fruits or consequences of one's actions; he agreed that humans are liable to a destiny according to their deeds. Tathagata Buddha declared human deeds as the cause of repeated (birth–death–rebirth; and accepted the deed itself as the basis of *Nirvana*. 'The Principle of the Four Noble Truths'—Arya Satya (*dukha*—suffering, source of *dukha*, cessation of *dukha* and path of cessation of *dukha*) expounded by him, shows first the mirror (fact) of human life and then provides point wise knowledge and intelligence to make it purposeful and fruitful. Not only has this, Gautama Buddha's call for determined adaptation and specific commitments and promises for development of ideal virtues, especially *shila*—the moral conduct (which is literally linked to calmness and pleasantness), also started virtually from individual life.

Shila turns a person virtuous and for this reason Lord Buddha has laid so much stress on it. A virtuous person can exercise self-control and then, as a key to all happiness and goodness, one can reach the depths of the nature of excellent conduct. He can progress on the path to salvation of himself and then of the entire universe.

In reality, one can start from self. By renunciation of evil, a person, while developing ideal virtues through his good deeds, leads on the path of self-welfare and reaches the stage of salvation; be establishes himself as the ideal for others, and then inspires others towards the road to salvation. An individual who is not able to proceed on the path of self-welfare to reach the ultimate cannot become on inspiration to others. This is the universal truth. Beginnings have to be made from the bottom, that is, from the level of the individual.

This is the crux of the teaching of the Hinayana. It contains the condition of first becoming the light for the welfare of the self. Hinayana's message is to show enormous light to others after making the self luminous and shining.

Hinayana Buddhism is a nucleus in the life of millions of people of Asia and the world in general and in country like Thailand in particular. It is a matter of great satisfaction that people have accepted Buddhism in their daily lives in the best possible manner through their casteless and equality-based society. Which *karuna*, hospitality, sincerity, readiness towards self-reliance, development by peaceful means, and a hard-working temperament are the main features.

The five precepts,[7] the three-fold training,[8] the law of karma and the four virtues for a good or ideal household life[9] are these great, exemplary and emulative principles,[10] which made the life of Thais worthy; their observance strengthen. Simultaneously, the Buddhism that is followed by individuals, communities, and societies, even according to time and space.

Moreover, how to show respect for other faiths, ideas, and views, can be learned from Thai people. We know that Hinayana Buddhism, today, is the state religion of Thailand. Even so the tolerance showed by Thais for others is exemplary; and this greatness, I believe, given dimensions, one after the other, to the development of their nation at various levels.

Today, we are witnessing unprecedented material advancement and globalization; these are the days of liberalization. World citizens are coming closer to one another in different walks of life. Day by day, the tempo of mutual understanding and cooperation is increasing. We are continuously proceeding to become members of the world family by facing numerous problems and difficulties on our way. In such a situation, the way shown by Lord Buddha, or in other words, Buddhism, or the Buddhist teachings, especially pertaining to self-beginning are fully capable to become the basis of resolving all problems, from the individual to the international level, and to strengthen the spirit of global understanding and cooperation. The more we come closer to them in our daily practices, the more we gain.

India and Thailand are two ancient nations that have been connected with each other for more than two thousand years, and Buddhism has played the most important role in this linkage. Today, in the day of globalization, India and Thailand must go together; it is the need of the hour.

If karuna can be the basis of cooperation and understanding at the individual level, the *panchasheela* can be a solid basis of mutual relations, cooperation, and understanding amongst nations and communities; it can also be the basis of conflict resolution from the local to the global level.

In addition, it can become the basis of the beginning of a new and historical chapter of economic, cultural, and political relations amongst the nations of the world in general, and between India and Thailand in particular.

NOTES

1. Before Gautama Buddha, as the Buddhist treatises indicate, other Buddhas like Dipankar, Mangal, Suman and Reot, too, propounded the same philosophy in their respective ages.
2. *Atta Vaggo*—The Self, *Dhammapada*, Ch. 12, No. 116.
3. Of the *Dhammapada* (*na paresam katakatam, attano va aavekkheyya katani aakastani cha*).
4. Ibid. (*aata ha va jitam seyyo yo chayam itata pajam, aatadassa pusassa nichcham sannotacharino; neva devo na gandhabbo na maro saha brahamana, jitam, aapa jitam kayira tatharupassa jantuno*).
5. *Aatanam evem pathamam pathirupe nivesayam, aathannamanusaseyya na kilisseyya pandito; attanache tatha kayira yathannamanussati, sudantovata dammetha aattahi kira duddamo.*

6. *Attahi attano natho ko dwinatho parosiya, attana va sudanten nathan labhati dullabham.*
7. *Panchasheela.*
8. *Triratna.*
9. *Garavasa-dharma.*
10. In this chain, four *Brahma Viharas*, four Virtues for social unity, ten principles (as duty) for a ruler and the Middle Path can also be mentioned.

The Heritage Parks of Sukhothai and Kamphaeng Phet—Remains of Brahmanical Sites and Artefacts

SATYAVRAT SHASTRI

Of the three Historical Parks situated not far from each other, Sukhothai, Kamphaeng Phet and Si Satchanalai declared as Heritage Sites by Unesco, only two, the Sukhothai Historical Park and the Kamphaeng Phet Historical Park have Brahmanical sites and the Brahmanical artefacts discovered from areas around them which are now housed in the Museums there and the National Museum, Bangkok. As many as fourteen images of Hindu gods like Śiva, Viṣṇu, Hari-Hara and goddess Umā have been found from the Brahmanical shrines of the Sukhothai Historical Park which except two are now housed in the National Museum, Bangkok. The two of Viṣṇu and Hari-Hara are in the Ramkamhaeng National Museum, Sukhothai.

SHRINES OF SUKHOTHAI

Thewālai Kaset Phiman/Ho Thewālai

It is mentioned in the Stone Inscription of King Li Thai of AD 1361. This records the placing of the images of Śiva and Viṣṇu in the shrine in AD 1339 for Brāhmaṇas to worship.

The Inscription reads:

> In 1271 Śaka, year of the Ox, on Friday, the 11th of the waxing moon of Āṣāḍha in the ṛkṣa of Purvāṣāḍha at sun rise the king (Phra Pada Kamrateng AN Sri Sūryavaṁśa Rāma Mahārājādhirāja) erected an image of Maheśvara and an image of Viṣṇu in the Devālaya Mahaksetra of this Mango Grove . . . for all the ascetics and the Brāhmaṇas to worship for ever. . . .
>
> Khmer language, Face 1, Lines 51-53

An important thing in this Thewālai, Devālaya, is the base of a hall where these images originally stood. The hall is in the Maṇḍapa shape with eight columns and is 12 metres wide. This ancient monument was excavated and restored in AD 1970.

A peculiarity of the monument, the Śiva shrine, is that it lies straight in the direction of the Śiva Cave which is at the top of a faraway mountain noticeable from there.

Wat Si Sawai

It is situated 300 metres south-west of Wat Mahāthāt and is surrounded with beautiful scenery. Interesting work of art in it is the main Prang that consists of three towers of Lopburi style. In its front there are two bases of Vihāras located next to each other and surrounded with bricks/slate boundary wall. The outer wall is of laterite. From its excavation and renovation fragments and antiques were found such as a lintel showing Viṣṇu stepping over the ocean, fragments of a bronze idol, a Liṅga and a Buddhist image of Lopburi style. King Rama VI of the Chakri dynasty visited this temple when he was the Crown Prince. He had found the image of Svayambhu (Śiva) in the Vihāra. Hence it is assumed that Wat Si Sawāi was once the ancient site of the Brahmana religion.

Some Hindu sculptures were discovered from Wat Si Sawāi. They are preserved now in the Ramakamhaeng Museum at Sukhothai. These are

(i) an image of Hari-Hara in bronze of Sukhothai art, foureenth-fifteenth century AD.
(ii) an image of Śiva in bronze, Sukhothai art, foureenth-fifteenth century AD.
(iii) torso of Śiva in stone
(iv) torso of Śiva in stone
(v) right arm of a deity

Taphadaeng Shrine

It is situated north of Wat Mahāthāt. Also called Phra Sua Muang Shrine, its architectural style is a copy of the Khmer art which exercised influence over Sukhothai during the reign of King Sūryavarman II of the twelfth century AD. An excavation here revealed significant sculptures such as a figure of Śiva and a goddess. According to their accessories and dress it looks typically a Khmer sculpture of the Angkor Wat art of around the eleventh century AD.

Wat Phra Phai Luang

This ancient site is situated in the northern part outside the town of Sukhothai. It is adjacent to the outer enclosure of Sukhothai with Phra Ruang crossing the eastern part. It is known as one of the significant ancient sites of Sukhothai because it demonstrates historical traces of art having existed before the establishment of the town of Sukhothai until the late Sukhothai period. The cluster of ancient sites in the middle is surrounded by two moats. The outer moat is square shaped with approximately one kilometre width on each side. The inner moat is smaller than the outer one. It looks as if there was no moat in the eastern part. There are three Prāngs or Prāsāds representing the three essences of the ancient site. This is because the style of these towers and the decoration are similar to the Khmer art of the reign of King Jayavarman II. In the thirteenth century AD these towers were the place of worship of the Hindus. This is because the fragments of an idol and a pedestal were found from here. Since King Jayavarman VII had a strong belief in Mahāyāna Buddhism, he renovated the towers and highlighted the pediment and the stucco illustrating the previous life of the Buddha.

Wat Phra Phai Luang

Located to the east of the northern gate and the outer rampart of Sukhothai, it is considered a group of ancient edifices of great significance because its buildings constructed in different phases have left impressive evidence of the evolution of Sukhothai art.

The oldest ancient monuments in this ancient temple are three buildings constructed in Prāsād form (imitating Hindu Śikhara Vimānas). At present two of them are still in existence with their bases only in sight. The remaining one in the north is adorned with stuccoed relief depicting the stories of the Buddha like at a Prasad at Wat Mahāthāt at Lopburi Province and a Pallial Prāsād at Angkor. In addition there are stuccoed reliefs depicting deities of Hinduism, such as an image of Śiva and an image of Brahmā. These help confirm the supposition that around the thirteenth century AD communities in Sukhothai had cultural contact with Khmers in the reign of King Jayavarman VII and were also associated with a town under the Khmer influence called Lavo (the present Lopburi Province). To the east of the Prāsād are located a Vihāra and a Chedi in pyramid shape with every sloping side decorated with superimposed receding porches which are similar to those of Kutkut Chedi in Lampun Province for enshrining the stuccoed image of the Buddha.

THE BRAHMANICAL ARTEFACTS IN THE RAMKAMHAENG MUSEUM

Among its many exhibits this museum at Sukhothai had some Brahmanical artefacts which, apart from those mentioned in connection with the description of the Thewalai Si Sawai are:

(i) a Śivaliṅga in sandstone, Lopburi art, eleventh-twelfth century AD.
(ii) pedestal of Liṅga or Yoni, Lopburi art, eleventh-twelfth century AD.
(iii) an image of Hari-Hara, Sukhothai art, fourteenth century AD.
(iv) an image of Viṣṇu, Sukhothai art, fourteenth century AD.
(v) a panel depicting Viṣṇu resting on the celebrated serpent Śeṣa with its seven hoods with seated Lakṣmī holding the feet of the Lord in her arms. From the navel of the Lord springs forth a lotus stalk with full-blossomed lotus on which Brahmā is comfortably seated in a posture of worship. With a little towards the side of the feet there is the figure of a recluse with matted hair and rosary who could be Śiva. If this surmise were to be correct, then the panel would be representing the entire Hindu Trinity which would distinguish it from a similar panel at Prāsād Panom Rung.

SHRINES OF KAMPHAENG PHET

About 65 km from Sukhothai the Historical Park of Kamphaeng Phet has a Hindu shrine, now in ruins, amidst a large number of Buddhist ones, called the Śiva shrine where the bronze statue of Śiva that is considered as one of the masterpieces of Thai art was found. The inscription at the base of it, written in Thai language in Sukhothai script states that 'this was set up by Śrī Dharma Aśoka Rāja, a Governor of Kamphaeng Phet in AD 1510 for protection of people and animals in the Kamphaeng Phet city and for the accrual of merit to the two former kings of Ayutthiyā'.

The head and the hands of the statue were cut and stolen by a German missionary in AD 1886 (during the reign of King Chulalongkorn or Rama V) which the police discovered at Bangkok harbour and were restored to it (the statue) in such a way that nothing of the vandalism in it is noticeable now.

Apart from the Śiva statue discovered from the Śiva shrine which now occupies a pride of place on the first floor of the Kamphaeng Phet National Museum, a couple of other Hindu images have also been discovered from Kamphaeng Phet's other sites like Wat Mahāthāt. They are the images of Viṣṇu or Narāi and a goddess (she may be Umā or Lakṣmī). There are also two or three broken pieces that a can be ascribed to the Rama story.

From what has been stated above, it would be clear that the heritage sites of Sukhothai and Kamphaeng Phet have remains of a number of Brahmanical shrines and artefacts, among the large number of the Buddhist ones, a good testimony to the peaceful coexistence of the Buddhist and Brahmanical religions in the kingdom of Thailand since days of yore. These also are a positive proof of the close and intimate Indo-Thai linkages down the ages.